MW01104402

LATE-BREAKING
AMAZING STORIES™

IDENTITY THEFT

The scary new crime that targets all of us

by Rennay Craats

Altitude Publishing

PUBLISHED BY ALTITUDE PUBLISHING LTD.
1500 Railway Avenue, Canmore, Alberta T1W 1P6
www.amazingstoriesbooks.com
1-800-957-6888

Publisher	Stephen Hutchings
Associate Publisher	Kara Turner
Canadian Editor	Brendan Wild
U.S. Editor	Julian S. Martin
Fact Checker	Andy Sayers

ALTITUDE GREENTREE PROGRAM
Altitude Publishing will plant twice as many trees as were used
in the manufacturing of this product.

In order to make this book as universal as possible, all currency
is shown in US dollars.

Cataloging in Publication Data
Craats, Rennay, 1973-
    Identity theft / Rennay Craats.

(Late breaking amazing stories)
ISBN 1-55265-301-3 (American mass market edition)
ISBN 1-55439-504-6 (Canadian mass market edition)

    1. Identity theft. I. Title. II. Series.

    HV6675.C73 2005   364.16'3   C2005-905271-6

Printed and bound in Canada by Friesens
2 4 6 8 9 7 5 3 1

"It's so very simple to be anyone you please, on any given morning you awake."

Identity thief
James Rinaldo Jackson

CONTENTS

Convicted computer hacker Kevin
Mitnick photographed in January 2000
on his release from jail. (For more on
the story of Kevin Mitnick see page 67.)

Warren Lambert from San Francisco displays a letter notifying him that his identity may have been stolen, February 23, 2005, following an attack on ChoicePoint Inc. (For more on the ChoicePoint story see page 98.)

Frank Abagnale Jr., author of the bestselling book about his life as a successful con-artist, *Catch Me If You Can*. The book was made into a movie starring Leonardo DiCaprio and Tom Hanks. (For more on Frank Abagnale see page 137.)

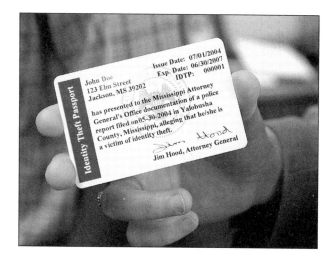

A demo identity card from Jackson, Mississippi, in July 2004. Issued by the attorney general's office to document victims of identity theft, the card was designed to help victims prove their true identities.
(For more about the difficulties facing victims of identity theft see page 78.)

CHAPTER 1

Introducing an Identity Thief

dentity thieves come in all shapes and sizes, ages and aptitudes. One thing they all share, however, is their ability to con people out of valuable information that allows them to then take over another person's identity. While some thieves target family members or neighbors, others shoot a little bit higher for bigger rewards. One identity thief from Memphis, Tennessee, a likeable and friendly man named James Rinaldo

Jackson, took on the names and then took over the bank accounts of a number of illustrious business executives and Hollywood high rollers. In the 1980s, Jackson started out staging car accidents for the insurance money, and he and his friends earned nearly $650,000 with about 50 fake accidents. While this was a lucrative business, it took a lot of time and effort to organize and execute. He wanted something bigger and better and faster, and a friend schooled him in the art of social engineering as a means to get information from people easily. This information, his friend told him, could net him a tidy profit through identity theft.

Jackson put his newly acquired education to the test and chose a victim essentially at random: he saw an interview with Gerald Levine of Time Warner on television, and this man seemed like a sufficiently wealthy first target. After Levine, Jackson chose a litany of other rich victims, many of whom he ripped from the pages of *Who's Who in America*. He deceived health companies into handing over confidential information and then took over his rich victims' identities to steal their money. In two years, Jackson had stolen from some of the biggest names in the corporate world, including Edward Brennan of Sears fame, and the former head of Chase Manhattan Bank, Charles Lebreque. One of the greatest of these early scams involved a real estate mogul named Jack Belz. Jackson stole mail from this Tennessee millionaire and was able to obtain a credit card in his name. He pulled in about $116,000 worth of merchandise and cash withdrawals on this card before the Belz family realized what was happening and put an end to Jackson's spending spree.

Throughout 1990, Jackson bought homes and fancy cars and created fraudulent credit cards in other names. In the process, he became a very wealthy man himself. He carried fake identification with him, and often used it to impress women with his claims of being an FBI agent or a U.S. Marshal. He used the same identification to avoid paying prostitutes he hired. At the end of the evening, Jackson would flash his badge and tell the ladies that it was a bust, but he offered to let them go if they returned the money he had paid them. In late 1990, Jackson's luck started to run out and the police closed in. He was arrested in 1991, and at the time he had a number of credit cards emblazoned with the names of the who's who of corporate America, along with thousands of fake driver's licenses. Even as he waited in jail to find out his fate, Jackson didn't rest and continued to obtain "impossible" information. Whether for fun or revenge, Jackson placed a telephone call to an emergency dispatch center, stating there was a domestic disturbance at the home of the FBI agent who had helped arrest Jackson and asked for help at the agent's address. Of course, the fact that the agent's address was thought to be a well-kept secret hadn't even slowed this master information thief. He also expressed his displeasure with Judge Julia Smith Gibbons' unwillingness to listen to Jackson's complaints about conditions in jail. He sent her a box of bugs he had trapped in his cell to drive home the point. Needless to say, these actions didn't help his cause and, instead, contributed to Jackson's sentence of seven years in prison. But that didn't mean his career as an identity thief was over.

In a time before the Internet was in every home and before famous people could more effectively protect their private information, Jackson managed to get a package to then movie studio CEO Terry Semel's unlisted home address. In 1993, he sent a package that contained Semel's confidential information: credit card data, Social Security number, and segments of his credit report. Then Semel found several other similar files in the package, including one for Mel Gibson, Steven Spielberg, and Danny DeVito. Semel was shocked to discover that he was looking at credit card statements, mothers' maiden names, and the bank account numbers of some of the most influential people in

Hollywood. Jackson told Semel that someone was going to commit fraud against these people, but maybe a movie deal for a hopeful screenwriter would help prevent that from happening. Semel, however, didn't take the package to heart and disregarded the screenwriter's claims. He had no way of knowing that the package had come from someone residing in a Millington, Tennessee, prison.

During the time that Jackson was collecting information on about 100 celebrities—from Tom Cruise to Arsenio Hall—he was an inmate in a federal institution. He used a cell phone he had smuggled in to find out information about people he admired. While he didn't want to cause them all damage, he was curious to see how people like Steven Spielberg lived. He first called the Screen Actors Guild to find out who provided health care insurance to the famous director. Then he spoke to the insurer claiming to be from a medical provider looking to confirm Spielberg's information. Jackson was able to find out Spielberg's Social Security number, address, and other personal information. Armed with this, he could social-engineer account information from American Express with a simple phone call. The representative that fielded the call asked if Jackson was "the" Steven Spielberg, and Jackson replied that he was not, but that he got that question all the time. After chatting with the representative for a few minutes and providing the real Spielberg's Social Security number and birth date, Jackson was able to monitor what Steven Spielberg bought on his American Express card over the course of a whole year and learned where the director ate, shopped, and what his card balance was every month. He didn't charge anything to the card; rather, he watched and admired the director's taste and spending habits.

This type of spying continued for some time, but not everyone got off as luckily as Steven Spielberg. While behind bars, Jackson was able to take over accounts and steal thousands of dollars from some of the richest people in the country. Fellow inmates helped Jackson by looking out for guards while the thief was on the telephone, and in return they enjoyed clothes, sneakers, jewelry, and food bought on credit cards he managed to take over. Then Jackson made a critical mistake. He tried to make too big a score at one time and set off alarm bells, which led to his being caught. His scams were finally discovered and Jackson earned himself another two years in jail—without phone privileges.

In 1998, Jackson was released from prison to find a con climate ripe for the picking. The Internet facilitated his criminal plans and led him to potential victims. He combed the online and newspaper obituaries for wealthy victims and collected information from online brokers that enabled him to steal hundreds of thousands of dollars from victims' bank accounts or to wire money out of these accounts to order diamonds and expensive jewelry from diamond merchants. Jackson wooed clerks at Fifth Third Bank in Ohio, the Bank of New Hampshire, American Express, and other institutions in order to obtain privileged information about his targets. He also used online information brokers, paying between $50 and $100 for vital pieces of information such as Social Security numbers. Jackson commonly changed the billing addresses for accounts and credit cards to keep his victims from quickly recognizing the theft had occurred, and he increased the credit limit of these credit cards so he could get the most out of the scams in a short time. Jackson even posed as his victims over the telephone—even though some of the victims were dead at the time of his fraud—to make wire transfers of large sums of money. There was little checking done on the other end to ensure the identity of the person on the phone was valid: Jackson was never asked for a password or personal identification number to verify his identity. Had he been, his criminal identity-theft career may have been much shorter and much less profitable. But Jackson had learned the practices of social engineering well, and he knew what to look for to get the best results. He listened for the voices of a young-sounding customer service agent on the other end: experience told him these employees were eager to help and lacked the experience to ask questions when doubtful. These newer employees didn't want to be reprimanded or fired for giving the company's wealthiest clients a hard time. If he found himself speaking with an older, wiser representative, Jackson often made an excuse to end the call and hung up, only to call back to try for someone more malleable.

These clerks were so agreeable that Jackson was able to make complicated transfers to jewelry brokers in exchange for approximately $750,000 worth of stunning diamonds and watches. He saw an advertisement for diamonds and decided impulsively that he needed to have the gems shown in the pictures. For approximately two months, he used the identities and bank accounts of recently deceased millionaires, including those of Dr. James Klinenberg, who had been the administrator of the Los Angeles' Cedars-Sinai Medical Hospital, and newspaper publisher Nackey Loeb, the CEO of Coca-Cola Enterprises, John Alm, and John Bollenback, CEO of Hilton Hotels. His shipments all went to hotels for pick-up, which didn't pose problems with the credit card companies because Jackson had already changed the billing addresses to match. Then Jackson sent an accomplice to the hotels to retrieve his packages. While clever, Jackson made some very crucial mistakes. He used many different names for the diamond orders, but he offered the same voice mail number for his contact number. Brokers, who are part of a very intimate industry, began talking about these transactions and became suspicious, as did FBI agents working the case. Again, the police began to move in on Jackson, and again he was arrested after picking up a package from a diamond wholesaler that was part of a sting operation. His incredible crime spree came to an abrupt end.

Despite the many thefts he committed, which netted hundreds of thousands of dollars in goods, the identity thief had virtually no money at the time of his arrest, and he had to have a defense attorney appointed by the courts. James Rinaldo Jackson, at age 41, pleaded guilty to 29 felony charges in 2000 and all that remained to be determined was the length of his prison sentence. The long-time identity thief claimed to be a compulsive gambler and that it was this addiction that drove him to steal identities and money. This defense didn't hold water (and Jackson later confessed it was untrue), so Jackson threw himself at the mercy of the court. The court, however, wasn't eager to cut the identity thief a break and sought to enhance his sentence to ensure he would serve as much time as possible. At his plea hearing, Judge Deborah Batts asked Jackson to tell her about his crimes. He was happy to talk, and he boasted about his exploits and how he pulled off pretending to be some of the richest people in the country. Jackson offered a play-by-play for the court record of every move he made and every detail of his extensive repertoire of identity thefts. In the process, he showed more pride than remorse, and Jackson's gift for the gab finally worked against him. He was sentenced to 80 years in prison.

Jackson's sentence was harsh because the court ruled he used "sophisticated means" to commit his crimes. His schemes were complicated and carefully planned: he accessed and changed credit lines, used courier services to deliver his stolen merchandise to various hotels to keep his distance from the transaction, and he used prepaid phone cards to avoid leaving a trail. The amount of money he stole—the huge losses suffered by his numerous victims—was an additional consideration in imposing the stiff sentence. In 2002, James Rinaldo Jackson appealed the sentence, saying it was unfairly enhanced and that his scams weren't sophisticated at all. But in 2003, the United States Court of Appeals rejected his claims and reaffirmed Jackson's original sentence.

The way in which Jackson carried out his thefts over the course of his 15- or 20-year career, as well as his famous victims, made him media fodder and a much studied criminal in law classes. It's no surprise, then, that James Rinaldo Jackson became one of the most infamous identity thieves in American history.

CHAPTER 2

The Issue

I dentity theft is a growing phenomenon across the globe, and you can scarcely pick up a newspaper or magazine without running across an article about some aspect of this crime: the scope of debit and credit card fraud, one company after another admitting their data banks have been compromised and personal information stolen, and scam e-mails defrauding people out of thousands of dollars. Even television commercials for corporations such as AOL, Citibank, and American Express bombard us with the threat of being cleaned out by an identity thief. While we'd like to chalk this up to fear mongering, the scary truth is that the concern and the media attention are warranted. This crime has topped the Federal Trade Commission's list of consumer complaints for years, and it has emerged as one of the most prolific white-collar crimes of this century—and it continues to get worse.

The Federal Bureau of Investigation defines identity theft as the "theft or misuse of personal or financial identifiers to gain value and/or facilitate criminal activity." The Identity Theft and Assumption Deterrence Act of 1998 makes it a federal crime when a person "knowingly transfers or uses, without lawful authority, a means of identification of another person with the intent to commit, or to aid or abet, any unlawful activity that constitutes a violation of federal law, or that constitutes a felony under any applicable state or local law." Acts of identity theft can violate other laws, adding more felony offenses to the crime. In some instances, cases can carry sentences of 30 years in prison and substantial fines and forfeitures. While Canada doesn't have a specific identity theft law, components of many of these cases lead to charges of fraud, impersonation, and uttering a forged document. So, with these deterrents in place, how can identity theft be growing?

It's simple, says Constable Kathy Macdonald of the Calgary Police Service's Crime Prevention Unit in Canada. "This type of crime [offers] very high return and a very low risk of getting caught," she says. And with the advancements in modern technology, the problem has become even more complicated in the 21st century. "What used to take place with someone stealing someone's identification and committing a fraud has now become multilayered, with a number of individuals being involved," says Staff Inspector Tony Crawford of the Toronto

Police Service Fraud Squad. The big pay-off of this crime, along with the different ways in which identification can be obtained and used, may explain why such a wide range of people commit this form of fraud: from opportunists that lift your wallet to a desperate family member, from a terrorist group looking to fund operations to organized crime groups seeking a lucrative scam.

The opportunists are people who hope to be in the right place at the right time. They slip in behind legitimate employees, or "piggyback," into secure buildings and restricted areas, and then roam around offices looking for an unattended laptop to steal, a wallet left in a jacket on the back of a chair, or even an unattended computer to hack into. Many of these opportunists dress the part: they wander the corporate halls sporting three-piece suits and briefcases. If anyone should question them, these thieves often pull a résumé out from under an arm and say they are looking for the Human Resources department to apply for a job. Thieves will also crash conventions and conferences in order to find what they need. You may leave your laptop on your chair for a few minutes while you grab a bite to eat from the buffet and return to find it missing. While some criminals are lone wolves, organized groups also target downtown hotels and conventional halls in order to relieve you of your valuables. These teams of criminals are smooth—meeting executives in airports, hotel lobbies, buffet lines, and restaurants. They distract you, often by spilling food or a drink on you or asking about where the cabs stop, or even troubling you for the time, and then they steal your luggage and laptop computer. These groups of two or three will stay in one city for a week, make the rounds at major hotels, and then travel to another city to start over again.

The loss of the laptop itself isn't the major concern. It's what's inside that can cause significant problems. Saved on the hard drive could be a number of sensitive documents.

People leave their wills saved on computers, store their résumé and banking information in computer files, keep address books on the hard drive, and save bids on corporate contracts. Not only can this information damage a corporate reputation if lost, it can put people at risk of identity theft. Simple steps can safeguard the information found on a work or personal laptop. There are several means to instantly encrypt data in a computer to keep it secure, and there are ways to trace your computer with programs such as CompuTrace and PC Call Home. Keeping a laptop in a traditional, recognizable laptop bag effectively advertises that you're carrying one. Using a more ambiguous carrying case can help ward off laptop-related identity theft. When it comes time to trade in a laptop, it's critical that you remove the hard drive or have it professionally wiped clean to prevent any information from falling into the wrong hands. And the most important advice of all? Keep an eye on your surroundings. Question strangers you don't think should be in a particular area. Otherwise, they can leave undetected from the office with its most valuable property: your identity.

Other opportunists may pick your pocket or steal your purse to make use of the identification kept inside. Once they have a victim's driver's license and a few other pieces of identification, thieves can easily open bank accounts or take out loans in another name. Key pieces of information for identity thieves include a victim's full name, address, date of birth, mother's maiden name, and a Social Insurance or Social Security number. They can, however, do quite well with much less to go on. Nonetheless, police departments urge people to slim down their wallets

TRADITIONAL THEFT

While high-tech methods of stealing information are in the headlines, a Javelin Strategy and Research study revealed that more than 68 percent of identity theft is committed offline. Stolen or lost wallets, stolen mail, and personal identification stolen by relatives or acquaintances were found to be the most common means of losing one's identity.

and to carry only essential pieces of identification—just in case. If there's a credit card that is not often used, it is best left at home. It's also advisable to carry a low-limit credit card in your wallet unless you know you are going to be making a large purchase. This minimizes the damage your card can inflict in the wrong hands. Memorize PIN codes rather than write them on a note in your wallet, and never carry a birth certificate or Social Insurance or Social Security card with you. Keep these pieces of identification in a safe place and take them with you only when you know you will need them. It's also a good idea to keep close track of everything carried in your wallet. Place each piece on a photocopier and copy it, front and back. Then, if your wallet is stolen or lost, you will know exactly what to cancel. "People cancel the driver's license and the credit cards, but they don't cancel a lot of those other cards—Sears, Safeway, Co-op cards, gas cards. In the hands of an identity thief, these few pieces in your name can be used to build a portfolio," warns Constable Macdonald. Using even "novelty" pieces of identification, like a library card or video store membership, thieves can fabricate a cache of identification in another name. It's easy to do. Just enter "fake id" into Google or another search engine on the Internet. It can deliver more than 2.2 million hits that offer quality fake identification, including driver's licenses, diplomas, and even Sheriff's badges.

There is another golden opportunity for identity thieves located right outside your door— your mailbox. This is a prime resource to mine nuggets of information about you. Mail theft, then, is a common and age-old means to steal someone's identity. Credit card applications are easy money because thieves can simply fill out the application, change the address, and wait for their new credit card to arrive in your name and with your bank information. You can opt-out of mail marketing lists and ask your banks not to send you pre-approved applications in order to limit the amount of potentially dangerous mail you receive. Bank statements, bills, government documents, driver's license renewals, and credit applications are great places to start for identity thieves. This mail provides thieves with your address, the name of your bank and account numbers, and canceled checks complete with your signature, driver's license number, and credit card limit. Armed with these tidbits, criminals can

U.S. MILITARY AT RISK

American soldiers are especially vulnerable to identity theft because each individual's Social Security number is printed on his or her military identification card. Soldiers also recite this number with their name and rank as their serial number. In addition, spending long periods of time away from home often means bank statements and mail are not received in a timely way or are not examined closely, leaving identity thieves considerable opportunity to defraud their victims.

quickly assume your identity and empty your bank accounts or set up lines of credit or credit cards in your name. Some will even fill out a change of address form at the post office to redirect your mail to an easier and less conspicuous location than your front step. Then they can examine your mail at their leisure, waiting for that one piece that will give them all they need to take over your name and your savings.

Keeping an eye on your mailbox is a great strategy to avoid being victimized. If a statement doesn't arrive, follow up immediately to ensure it wasn't taken from your mailbox. If you have ordered new checks from the bank or are expecting a replacement credit or debit card, be sure to call if it doesn't arrive when it should. In the case of mass reissues, cards can go missing or be stolen at the post office as well, so staying on top of these matters can make all the difference. Better still, people should arrange to pick up these items—bank issues, birth certificates, passports, and the like—whenever possible to eliminate the possibility of mail theft in the first place. To help reduce the chances of being victimized in this way, police urge people to empty their mailboxes regularly or even to install a lock on the box to keep thieves out. Also, mail your letters and payments from secure boxes rather than leave them on the counter at the office to be picked up—couriers, visitors to the office, or even other employees can be tempted to grab your mail from the bin and use the information inside against you. Vigilance and attention can make the difference between keeping your identity safe and finding out too late that you have become a victim.

But sometimes it's not the incoming mail that can ignite an identity thief's imagination. Instead, it can be the mail you discard that gives a thief all he or she needs to take over your identity. Because mail is a hot commodity in identity theft, "dumpster diving" can be a lucrative career and render huge amounts of information. Methamphetamine users are popular recruits for this sort of work and many use it to finance their drug habits. "When they are binging on methamphetamine, they are awake 24 hours a day for two weeks at a time," says Calgary

Police Service's Constable Macdonald. Dumpster divers sift through garbage in both commercial and residential areas and look for something useful, especially in garbage from hotels, rental car businesses, and other companies that swipe credit cards for reservations and then discard them once the customer has paid. While they are supposed to shred them, many companies simply throw these copies in the trash, and thus open the opportunity for identity thieves to access those precious accounts. As well, garbage bags that contain unwanted applications for credit cards or lines of credit, along with any personal statements, are goldmines for these thieves.

While a good start, even shredding material is not always a guarantee that information won't end up in the wrong hands. "Meth users have been known to tape those long strands of shredded material back together, so cross-cut shredders are really important," warns Macdonald. After all, methamphetamine users are extremely detail-oriented during binges and can use their days of wakefulness to put those paper puzzles back together. An inexpensive crosscut shredder is a good option for peace of mind and safety.

Tombstone Thieves

No one is exempt from becoming a victim of identity theft, even the dearly departed. That's why it should come as no surprise that tombstone identity rings are also common. These opportunists troll newspapers or cemeteries for victims, rather than office buildings. Hollywood is no stranger to these types of identity thefts: *Day of the Jackal* finds the main character taking on the identity of a deceased person. *The Talented Mr. Ripley* sees the same event unfold. For real-life scenarios, obituary sections are rich fodder for thieves, because they offer up dates of birth, full names, and often family information that can prove valuable for identity criminals. After collecting some basic information, thieves can create accounts, amass debts, and leave large loans unpaid, all in the deceased's name. While family members have little trouble proving their loved ones were not responsible for these charges and accounts, it is a shock to have to deal with creditors at such a painful time. In some cases, people with terrible credit are using the deceased's good credit to co-sign loans. In Atlanta, Kwezeta Butler sold the identities of 80 recently deceased people for $600 each, and these names and information were used to secure car loans totaling $1.5 million.

James Rinaldo Jackson, a career identity thief, obtained information about extremely wealthy people who had recently passed away, including Gordon Teter, CEO of Wendy's Restaurant. Jackson simply called the funeral home claiming to be Teter's insurance company and asked for some information to complete his report. He was given a Social Security number, date of birth, and address during that phone call. Another phone call, this time to Wendy's head office, garnered Jackson the name and location of Teter's bank, and yet another call to the bank secured him Teter's account and credit card numbers. Then all that was left was to withdraw Teter's money from his account. With little more than a smooth telephone manner and a newspaper, Jackson was able to pull off this and similar scams against the estates of many well-off people. Impersonation of the dead is a growing area of identity theft around the world and is Great Britain's fastest growing identity crime. In 2004, 70,000 British families experienced this type of fraud, causing grieving loved ones more pain and unnecessary aggravation. These statistics are only growing, both overseas and in North America.

Authorities urge people to omit a loved one's birthdate in an obituary to make identity thieves' work more difficult. As well, family members should notify credit card companies, banks, and other relevant organizations immediately so they are aware that the individual has died and will not request additional accounts.

Identity Thieves, Big and Small

In many cases, an identity theft ring is actually a network of thieves that target large data banks of information to find a large number of victims all in one place. Where terrorist groups may have used the drug trade to finance their activities before, many have switched to identity theft to get their money. This form of crime gives thieves a large return in a hurry while they remain relatively safe from arrest or conviction—a perfect option for these cells. The possibility of garnering large sums of money aside, stealing identities gives terrorists different names they can hide behind as they carry out illegal acts. They can operate in a different country using stolen and fraudulent driver's licenses, passports, birth certificates, and student visas. Even without exceptional skill or knowledge, today's technology and graphic design programs, paired with quality printers, allow criminals to create superb counterfeit documents and identification. This threat is something authorities are mindful of around the world.

While terrorists make up a small percentage of identity thieves, the same can't be said for another criminal group. "For the most part, the bulk of theft is organized crime. They are data mining and then using that data to try to get credit cards and so on, and then buying products to sell to get cash. Then they are shipping it out of the country," says Detective Staff Sergeant Barry Elliot, coordinator at PhoneBusters, Canada's national anti-fraud call center. These organized crime groups work in many different ways, from small networks that steal laptops to gain information, to larger groups that hack into data banks to steal hundreds or even thousands of files at one time.

For any identity thief, whether a part of an organized group or not, employees are the key to a successful operation. Many employees have access to a plethora of important information, and if thieves can get to these people, their job becomes much easier. Employees are any company's greatest assets, but these days they can also be the greatest liabilities. Employees can be tricked into releasing information, conned into releasing information by a smooth talker on the other end of the telephone. If the person answering the phone is privy to

STUDENT AID FRAUD

Identity thieves have targeted the United States Department of Education federal student aid programs, which processes more than 11 million aid applications and grants more than $60 billion per year in aid funding. Thieves submit fraudulent loan applications under assumed names. In one case, a man used more than 50 different identities, many of which belonged to prison inmates, and was awarded $313,000 in student aid funding.

everything that goes on at the company, the entire system can be at risk. What are the solutions? "Limit collection of data and limit the keys to the kingdom," says Constable Macdonald. Not everyone needs passwords and access to material and information, especially confidential and sensitive information. Further, companies need to have secure hiring and firing practices in place—they should conduct background checks so they know who is working for them and thus safeguard the security of information. By paying attention to how material is shredded, how it is recycled or disposed of, and circulating manuals regarding anti-theft procedures and guidelines, management can head off potential problems before they occur.

In some cases, employees are not deceived. Instead, they are disgruntled or desperate for money, and they seize the opportunity to exploit their company for cash. They decide to steal and sell their clients' personal information to the highest bidder. "Your name is housed in so many different institutions you have no control over the security. You can shred your stuff, but really your biggest risk is through a corrupt employee at an institution where your name is housed," says PhoneBusters coordinator Barry Elliot. Some high-profile cases of low- to mid-level employees cashing in on confidential information have raised the alarm and made companies look at internal security differently. They are also looking to government agencies to do more. The problem is, says Toronto Police Service Fraud Squad's Staff Inspector Tony Crawford, the laws don't do all they should or could to protect people. "In Canada, stealing information from a computer is a criminal offense if it's done by accessing data that [a person doesn't] have a particular right to. Recording information by writing it on a piece of paper and taking that information with them is not a criminal offense," Crawford says. This creates a loophole—and serious problems and frustration for victims. Many of the information files held in large data banks contain extensive personal information and puts the people behind these files at great risk. In these circumstances, there is very little people can do to protect themselves because their security is in the hands of the people working at these data banks and large corporations. In one case, a person was arrested after stealing information about 115,000 people and selling that chunk of names to the highest bidder on the street. Another man stole information from his mortgage customers and then opened up gambling accounts for himself in their names. He also peddled the information to identity theft rings for extra money.

Gone Phishing

The information age launched by the Internet may be providing data to the wrong people. The Internet is proving a useful tool for criminals who scam people out of their most prized possession: their identities. The prevalence of e-mail in today's society opens the door for identity thieves to take advantage of the instant nature of the communication. They count on the ease with which people can act on e-mail messages to ensure the success of their schemes. One of the newest and fastest growing scams is called phishing (pronounced fishing), and it is a great example of using urgency and panic to steal people's information. These unsolicited e-mails claim to be sent from a reputable financial institution, retail company, government agency, or other business, and they alert you to a serious problem with your account. Organizations including Charter One, SouthTrust, Royal Bank, CIBC, PayPal, and e-Bay have all been used by fraudsters to create phishing e-mails. Some of these messages inform customers of a scheduled software upgrade and ask that recipients visit the link provided to confirm their data to ensure no loss of service. Messages more often warn of a recent security breach against the company's network and ask that customers immediately log onto a link conveniently provided in the message to update or verify their information. This step, the e-mail asserts, is the only way to guarantee that customers aren't affected by this breach. In truth, the link takes the victim to the criminal's page, which is designed to look just like the real company's site. The phishers use copied corporate logos, graphic elements, and other information found on the legitimate web sites to convince victims of their authenticity. Then victims are prompted to verify account information including ATM card numbers and PIN codes, credit card numbers and expiry information, and the card holder's full name, address, and date of birth. Some phishing sites will instead provide wrong numbers that need updating and allow you to correct them with authentic account information. Others will simply ask you to input your passwords and credit card number or account details. In some cases, phishing scams have incorporated computer worms and viruses that spread the phishing e-mails to even more people through victims' e-mail address books. And if you reply to these messages, you may well find yourself on a list that is circulated among phishers. Then other identity scams and e-mail messages, prompting you to act quickly to prevent disaster, will appear in your inbox with greater frequency and volume.

Phishing schemes can violate a number of laws, including identity theft, wire fraud, credit card fraud, and bank fraud laws, as well as the CAN-SPAM Act (Controlling the Assault of Non-Solicited Pornography and Marketing Act) of 2003 in the United States. Phishing is worrying the business world as well. IBM Corp., a services company that tracks worldwide security threats, reported that instances of phishing reached a record high in May 2005 as massive numbers of scam e-mails were disseminated to inboxes across North America and around the world. Perhaps victims and criminals alike were responding to headline after headline screaming about the pervasive and spreading nature of identity theft around the globe. While the majority of phishing sites are operated out of the United States, the Anti-Phishing Working Group reported 68 different countries hosted phishing sites, with more than 2,850 active sites in April 2005 alone. The sites incorporated nearly 80 different legitimate company brand names in their scams.

There are some dead giveaways that the e-mails aren't on the up-and-up: obvious spelling errors; the fact that you, the recipient of the e-mail, are not even a customer of the company in question, and other inconsistencies within the message. Regardless, many people are enticed by the urgent nature of the e-mail messages and succumb to the panic that their financial security may be at risk and thus fall victim to these phishing expeditions.

Pharming (also known as domain spoofing) is another sophisticated and complicated scam that identity criminals are beginning to add to their arsenals. Unlike phishing, pharming sites allow people to come to them. While it is not the site you want to visit or think you are connected to, pharming sites provide believable spoof sites to make you think you are at the right place. Each Internet address is made up of a row of numbers. Instead of having to remember these numbers to access a given web site, a search engine and server translate those numbers for users and then automatically connect them to the corresponding web site. But identity thieves involved in pharming change the string of numbers related to a specific web site (most often financial web sites) and redirect users to their own fraudulent web site location.

To the user, the URL and the site will commonly look fine—there will often be no evidence of the hijack or any other discrepancy. So, while there, users are comfortable inputting personal information to log on or conduct transactions, and the identity thief captures it keystroke for keystroke. Unlike phishing e-mails and sites, potential victims often don't suspect anything on pharming sites because they were not solicited in the first place. "The chances of getting more people fooled is greater than with phishing, so pharming is more detrimental," says Constable Macdonald. These sites are hard to identify and have taken identity theft to another frightening dimension.

Reshipping

It seems too good to be true. A company wants to hire you for generous pay—sometimes $3,000 to $6,000 per week, or 15 percent of each package's value—to work from home and simply reship goods. The "employer" will send you small electronics such as cameras, personal digital assistants (PDAs), and laptop computers and all you have to do is repackage and reship them abroad. Some will also send wire transfers for auction goods to the new employee and require him or her to forward the funds to another account. But before this ridiculously easy job begins, the company requests that you fill out the basic paperwork to get you on the payroll: the usual personal information, including your Social Security or Social Insurance number, date of birth, address, and full name. The check amounts sent to you are often more than what was owed, and the company instructs its employee to cash it and forward the balance to an overseas account. Everything seems fine until the "company" bounces a check or submits an invalid cashier's check. In short order, the bank realizes that the check is no good and the employee is on the hook for the total amount. "In the meantime, you've been reshipping all sorts of stolen property for them and now you've been put out of pocket for shipping, too," says Constable Macdonald. The goods were purchased by stolen credit card information, often obtained through information acquired on phishing sites. The entire scheme falls apart and the employee learns he or she was not only scammed, but is also often the victim of identity theft. In the four or six weeks that you've been working for this company, the person behind it has opened bank accounts and taken out loans using your personal information. This type of fraud—a mixture of credit card fraud, identity theft, and auction fraud—is responsible for millions of dollars in losses each year.

Reshipping can also be set up over the Internet on chat rooms or bulletin boards for job postings. In some cases, criminals will develop a relationship with someone they met in a chat room and then reel their victim in with a story about his or her country not allowing direct business shipments from North America. So, now that they are friends, the thief asks to use the victim's address to receive these goods and for the victim to then reship the materials with the residential return address. After weeks of this, the victim is contacted by merchants saying the goods he or she has been shipping were bought with counterfeit or stolen credit cards. While not a case of direct identity theft, this arm of reshipping victimizes unsuspecting people and makes them unwitting criminals themselves.

Drive-by Identity Theft

Modern technology has given society fantastic devices that aim to make our lives easier and more convenient. Unfortunately, if used inappropriately, they can endanger our security. Wireless technology is a prime example of an advancement that helps identity thieves do their jobs. Wireless systems allow households to have several computers running in a network—in this way, all members have their own system and can use the computer and Internet at the same time. The downside is that if you aren't taking the proper steps to protect yourself and your computer network, you can become a victim.

Many identity thieves drive around neighborhoods sniffing out unprotected signals in the air. All it takes is a computer, a wireless Ethernet card, software that is readily available on the Internet, and a way to meander down streets until signals are detected. Some more sophisticated war drivers have an antenna and global positioning system (GPS) to facilitate their search and to allow the thieves to be farther away from the target but still receive the signals. Then they steal your bandwidth and, in the best-case scenario, share your Internet connection. The worst-case scenario involves these hackers accessing your computer and all the information saved on it. Black hat hackers, or malicious war drivers, snoop out passwords and gather information from vulnerable systems. "Then they may put it in a magazine called *2600* magazine. It has special passwords, codes, and different areas where you can steal bandwidth," says Constable Macdonald. Three times each year, this magazine publishes articles about everything to do with hackers, from writing code to government issues. Black hat hackers can pilfer passwords and use them to find out everything about you from your computer—including bank and credit information. At a minimum, wireless users should have WEP (Wired Equivalent Privacy) encryption and a firewall to keep undesirables out of their hard drive. The standard anti-virus and spam blocker programs are a must as well for any computer user.

War drivers are nothing if not courteous to one another. If they hit the jackpot, they aren't afraid to share with their friends to save them the trouble of scanning around. Based on the old hobo visual language of the 1930s that spread the word about nasty railroad police, gave directions, warned about mean dogs in the area, or tipped people off about where to find food, the 21st century version alerts war drivers to an open network or lets them know not to waste their time in a certain area. If there's an open network, war drivers draw a chalk circle with two semi-circles inside it on the side of a building or sidewalk. If it's a closed network, they'll place an X in the center of the circle. If there is WEP encryption, war drivers let their friends know by writing a W in the circle. In some areas, war drivers use the Latin words for war (*bellum*) and peace (*pax*) to get the word out. If the signal is open they write *bellum*, and if it is protected drivers write *pax*. These hackers will often update these signals as conditions in the area change. What likely looks like strange graffiti to most people is actually underground communication that could cost someone his or her identity.

Skimmers and Other Handy Devices

A phenomenon called skimming is causing huge problems for the banking industry and making credit card and ATM card users feel vulnerable. It only takes a second to steal all of your information from these trusted cards—and it can take place so quickly that you won't even notice it happening right in front of you.

All the personal information linked to your credit and ATM cards, including your name, address, and account numbers, are found on the magnetic strip on the back. With a simple tool called a wedge or a skimmer, which is about the size of a credit card, identity thieves can capture the information on the strip and later download it into a computer. Often, thieves will sell the filled up skimmer to someone else who will use the information to turn those files into victims. Waiters and cashiers working in restaurants and attendants at service stations provide ideal opportunities for criminals using wedges to collect people's personal information—they have access to their cards for a short time and can easily swipe the card without anyone knowing it.

These small electronic devices, which are sold legally, can be attached to the back of a waiter's apron with Velcro or affixed under a counter at a gas station for convenient access when needed. When you leave your credit card on the table to pay for dinner, or hand the card over rather than go into a store to pay for gas, these employees can complete the legitimate transaction you see on your statement. With an extra swipe through a wedge or skimmer, however, they can also hijack your account information. This sets the ball in motion for thieves to steal your identity or make unauthorized charges to your credit card. Wedges can hold up to 200 numbers, so thieves can amass a great deal of data in a short period of time. "Then they get the plastic, holographs, new printers— everything they need to make a secondary card," says Constable Macdonald.

In many cases, victims unknowingly do the swiping for identity thieves. Some sophisticated groups use expensive portable readers that fit snugly onto legitimate ATM card slots along with tiny high-resolution cameras hidden in brochure holders aimed at the machine's keypad. The electronic devices read the card and pull the number from it and the camera films as victims enter their PINs. Victims insert their cards and try to enter their PINs a few times but nothing happens: at least nothing the victims can see. In fact, thieves have already captured their information. Victims give up, assuming the ATM is out of order and leave to try another machine. Thieves often sit close to the ATM and record the transmission from the compromised machine. Once the thieves have enough information, they remove the device and set up again at a different ATM location. In Calgary, Canada, a group of sophisticated thieves entered the city in 2004 and after only an hour they were able to steal 35 customers' information. This crime is a lucrative means to commit bank fraud and, potentially, identity theft.

Smooth Talkers

We are all on guard against identity theft and try to do our part to avoid becoming victims: shredding documents, being responsible with our credit cards and debit cards, and being wary of Internet transactions and requests for information. How can it be, then, that one of the most widespread ways that thieves gather information about us to commit identity crimes involves getting it straight from the source? We give it to them. Social engineers trick us out of personal information by pretending to be employees at companies with which we may or may not have accounts, or by pretending to conduct

telemarketing surveys that require certain pieces of information. Some will even come to you
with a problem and ask for help.

One social engineer knocks on doors saying his wife is pregnant, his car has broken
down, and he needs $50 to pay a tow truck.
He leaves his driver's license, which is phony,
and promises to return in a few hours to repay
the kind loan. Of course, the fraudster doesn't
return and it's only after the neighbors begin
to talk that they realize they were all duped.
On a larger scale, Nigerian letter scams are
social engineering at its best. A letter or e-mail
from supposed Nigerian politicians, business
leaders, or even royals of that country state that
they are being victimized by a corrupt nation.
They have a large sum of money that they need
your help to get out of the country and they
plan to transfer money, often millions, into your
account. All you have to do is pay a few upfront
fees for taxes, attorney fees, bribe money, and
the like. In the end, the scam is revealed and

the victims lose their money. While these particular social engineers don't steal our identities, they demonstrate the power of persuasion in cons and scams. Persuasiveness comes in very handy when identity thieves put social engineering to work in their schemes to steal personal information.

Social engineers obtain information from you by first providing you with some basic information. These smooth operators often target children and young adults with their schemes to get information. Children are more likely to participate in online or telephone surveys, especially those that offer a small reward for taking part. "Kids will give out lots of information because they are going to get a case of soda or $20," says Constable Macdonald. And they don't realize or understand the consequences of revealing personal information, making them willing and pliable targets. Social engineers may call and ask the person answering the telephone to take part in a survey in which they may ask about his or her children, their names, and when they were born. Maybe they ask about a victim's heritage or genealogy to uncover your mother's maiden name or even ask if you have pets and what their names are. Some engineers will claim to be an employee of an insurance company or other organization and ask for information about an account or the account holder. In other cases, these criminals will say they are calling from a Do-Not-Call registry, or even an anti-fraud organization, and invite potential victims to sign up for the program. In return, they need to gather some information to ensure they are speaking with the correct person. Some of the requested information seems harmless on its own, but it can provide identity thieves with possible passwords and PIN codes that can then allow them to access accounts and masquerade as you. Revealing other information, like Social Security or Social Insurance numbers and financial information, can be devastating.

One well-known social engineer and computer hacker named Kevin Mitnick had been committing computer and wire crimes from the age of 17 before he alerted the authorities' interest for stealing information (and computer code) from various large corporations. When he was caught, Mitnick fled prosecution for two years with the FBI hot on his trail. During this time he drastically changed his routine and lifestyle and used new identities to evade police. When he was finally caught, Mitnick spent 59 months in prison on a 25-count indictment: Mitnick insisted he was innocent of some of these charges. "Mitnick isn't a thief or a terrorist. He's a recreational hacker. He didn't do it for economic gain or damage anything, and there's no allegation that he attempted to damage anything," his attorney, Donald Randolph, told CNN Interactive's John Christensen. Mitnick did what he did as part of a fun hobby and never profited from his social engineering. This game focused more on seeing what he could do and to expose the flaws in major corporations' security, often with the help of duped employees. Mitnick told *60 Minutes*' Ed Bradley in 2000 that he was able to compromise computer software design company Novell's security within minutes and that he stole source codes for high-tech cell phones from Motorola simply by social engineering an employee into e-mailing it to him. He could have easily stolen millions of dollars, but for him that was against the spirit of hacking. Authorities didn't see it that way and argued that Mitnick left systems vulnerable and information exposed, costing corporations millions to revamp their security networks.

The notoriety and media fervor the case generated made Mitnick a hacker idol and social engineering guru. His 2003 book, *The Art of Deception: Controlling the Human Element of Security*, tells of his experiences with social engineering and how easy it was to get someone to trust him and then use that trust to get what he wanted. Although Mitnick was a wizard on the computer, many of his techniques were applied over the telephone, not the computer. Although he exposed security problems in several companies, he claims, since his release from prison in 2000, he is reformed. He is now dedicated to education and making computer security more effective. His advice is simple: verify information, put people on hold to check out what they are telling you, never give out information, and confirm that the call is genuine before you proceed with it. After all, the best corporate security doesn't mean a thing in the face of bad judgment by human beings.

I Spy

It is amazing how many different people know what you are doing when you are on the Internet: marketers track your movements, parents monitor their children's access to web sites, company management watches where employees are surfing on company time. Tiny hidden files (called web bugs) keep close track of where you go while on the Internet. Numerous programs can also be attached to your computer system to watch and sometimes manipulate what happens on your computer. Spyware is everywhere. It is often to blame for a system slowdown, for crashes that have no explanation, and those annoying pop-up ads and spam messages. Spyware is programming that helps gather information about an individual or an organization without the person's or group's knowledge. Some nefarious spyware programs are designed to run software on your computer that allows it to collect PIN codes, banking identifications, credit card numbers, and other financial information. In fact, criminals using these systems can essentially do anything you can do—without needing to sit in front of your monitor.

Spyware is a tricky entity and one that, in some cases, we invite into our computers. Some web sites have user agreements to which the majority of people click "I agree" rather than read screens and screens of text. Within that agreement can be the permission to install spyware on your computer. From here, the sky is the limit for identity thieves. Firewalls, anti-virus programs, and anti-spyware programs all work in tandem to help protect users from insidious spyware.

Internet Information

Some of the "spying" that contributes to identity theft can be done through legitimate web sites. Even conducting a cursory Google search can turn up information about a potential victim. Other sites, including locator pages and superpage sites, can unearth information helpful to fraudsters. There are thousands of sites—some of which are offered free, while others are paid sites—that contain personal information about all of us. Genealogy sites such as FamilySearch.org operate huge databases that include death records as recent as 10 days old, birthplaces, and even Social Security numbers. Some sites offer court records, registrations, and background searches.

NetDetectiveSoftware.com and Docu-Search.com are two resources that contain detailed information, some of which is held by the FBI, that identity thieves can access for less than $200. "[Identity theft] absolutely is the simplest crime. Anyone can find out at least 22 pieces of information about you instantly, including your Social Security number, your mother's maiden name, someone who lives in your house who isn't related to you, and who lives around you in your neighborhood," says former fraudster-turned-consultant and the inspiration behind the movie *Catch Me if You Can*, Frank Abagnale Jr.

There are also sites and products like PrivacyGuard.com and Identityguard.ca that aim to protect people from identity thieves. These sites and products monitor credit and notify users immediately of any activity on a credit report.

You're a Victim: Now What?

Many people discover that they are victims of identity theft only after applying for a loan or requesting a copy of their credit report in anticipation of a major purchase. Because thieves can commit a number of crimes with your identity—from taking out loans to getting a job and filing fraudulent tax returns in your name—victims need to be thorough. Once the initial shock wears off, victims need to act quickly to prevent further damage to their credit and accounts. The United States Department of Justice and the Department of the Solicitor General, as well as Canadian law enforcement, urge victims to immediately do three things.

First, victims should inform their bank and credit card companies of the crime. Canceling affected accounts and then placing safeguards and passwords on new accounts can help minimize damage. Victims should contact all institutions by telephone and in writing to keep a paper trail of everything they do in relation to this crime. It's also important that victims keep complete records of their own to show what they have done, who they contacted, and the result of that contact—the process can take months or even years, so victims can't expect to remember every detail about what they did, what happened, and when.

Next, they should report the theft to their local police department and obtain a case number to aid with tracking the case's progress and information. Victims should request a copy of the report to add to their own incident file. This diligence can aid victims when dealing with creditors who require proof of the crime in order to process the claim.

Lastly, victims need to report the case to the appropriate private and government entities to cancel identification documents such as a driver's license and to request a flag be put on their files in case someone attempts to obtain identification in their names. Victims should also notify organizations, including the

Federal Trade Commission Identity Theft Hotline in the United States and PhoneBusters, the Canadian Anti-fraud Call Centre, and credit reporting agencies such as TransUnion, TransUnion Canada, Equifax and Equifax Canada, and Experian about any identity theft. Credit report agencies will apply fraud alerts to victims' credit reports to prevent someone else from opening accounts in their name. Initial fraud alerts stay on a victim's report for at least 90 days and extended alerts are kept for 7 years.

With the prevalence of identity theft in North America, many organizations have standard forms and letters that victims can fill out when reporting a theft, both online and in paper form. This ensures that people provide the correct information and the documents guide victims through the daunting process of filing and reclaiming their name. The Federal Trade Commission provides an Identity Theft Complaint form and an Identity Theft Affidavit to collect information about the victim and the crime and to file a complaint with the organization. PhoneBusters offers victims a similar Identity Theft Statement that not only gathers information but also provides the names, and in some cases phone numbers, of organizations to help victims determine who needs to know about the identity theft.

In cases of criminal identity theft in which a thief has used a victim's name during an arrest, it's likely that the victim's name is the one that will appear in the criminal records database. Now victims need to clear their names from this false criminal record by first contacting the arresting office or department and explaining that it was a case of misidentification. Procedures vary from area to area, but victims commonly have to prove their own identity and then file an impersonation report to get the identity crime on the record. Then they go through the courts to clear the court record as well. Victims should also request a letter clearing them of the charge, which victims should then carry with them at all times to avoid future incidents of mistaken identity.

CHAPTER 3

Celebrity Thieves

In most situations, the general public doesn't hear much about the main characters involved in identity theft. In some cases, however, identity thieves set their sights on well-known identities: those of celebrities. In some instances, the thieves themselves also gain notoriety for their gutsy criminal actions. A brazen identity thief took over the name of one Eldrick Woods, more commonly known as the professional golfer and advertising icon Tiger Woods. It seems unbelievable that someone would be able to steal the identity of this two-time Sports Illustrated Man of the Year, but Anthony Lemar Taylor did just that. With a Sacramento, California, driver's license bearing the athlete's name, 30-year-old Taylor was able to get store credit cards at several locations, all in Woods' name and attached to his credit. Between August 1998 and August 1999, Taylor charged around $17,000 worth of televisions and stereos, a used Lexus, furniture, and other goods to these cards, leaving Tiger Woods with the bills. Taylor was found guilty of eight felony theft and perjury charges related to these crimes, and due to his previous

STARTING YOUNG

At the age of 17, Abraham Abdallah, who would become the identity thief who targeted *Fortune* magazine's wealthiest people, had already started his career. He stole the identity of a stockbroker and withdrew chunks of $50,000 at a time from the broker's bank account to buy luxury sports cars and real estate.

convictions of robbery he was sentenced under California's "three strikes" law. The young man was sentenced to 200 years in prison in April 2001.

In other cases, the identity thieves are people close to celebrities. In June 2005, *American Idol's* Ruben Studdard announced that he was suing his former manager on charges of identity theft and forgery. He claims that his ex-manager, Ronald W. Edwards, forged documents that gave him power of attorney over the singer. Studdard also says that Edwards used his credit cards to rack up $105,000 in charges and wrote forged checks for $150,000. Of those checks, $22,000 worth were stolen and then deposited in Edwards's bank account. Amazingly, this all came to pass after Studdard sued Edwards in February 2005 for misusing nearly a quarter-million of the crooner's dollars.

Losing Yourself

In some cases, identity theft victims become

advocates for change because of their experiences. Michelle Brown became such an advocate. She addressed the United States Senate Committee Hearing on the Judiciary Subcommittee on Technology, Terrorism, and Government Information in July 2000. Her story also inspired a *Lifetime* network movie called *Identity Theft: The Michelle Brown Story*, starring Kimberly Williams-Paisley and Annabella Sciorra. As the facts of her battle against an identity thief unfold, it is indeed a plotline worthy of Hollywood. On January 12, 1999, this 28-year-old California woman found out someone else was using her name. Over the course of more than a year, this identity thief purchased in excess of $50,000 in merchandise and services, had rented properties, and used Brown's name when arrested for criminal misdeeds.

It began in January of 1998 when Brown applied to rent a property. The identity thief, Heddi Larae Ille, stole the application from the management office and used the information thereon to establish a wireless and then a residential telephone account, the balance of which was left at $1,443. Then Ille applied for timeshare financing and a store credit card but was denied. In October, Ille had a duplicate driver's license made in Michelle Brown's name but with a different address. "The requirement of her fingerprint enabled the authorities to clearly distinguish our different identities and made things much easier for me to clear my credit and to clearly establish the fact that I was the victim of identity fraud and impersonation," Brown told the Senate Committee in a written statement on July 12, 2000.

Ille then rented two properties in Brown's name and bought a $32,000 Dodge Ram pick-up truck and even underwent $4,800 worth of plastic surgery, paid for by a line of credit in Brown's name. In January 1999, a Bank of America employee shocked Brown when she called about a vehicle she was supposed to have bought. Brown realized she was a victim of identity theft. She promptly placed fraud alerts on her account through credit agencies, canceled her credit cards, imposed security measures on her bank accounts, and contacted the Department of Motor Vehicles, the police, and various government agencies to inform them of the breach. She did everything she was supposed to do—she filed all the right papers, made the appropriate phone calls, and stayed on top of developments in her case. During the roughly 500 hours she spent figuring out what had happened, she discovered some disturbing things about her identity thief that would directly affect Michelle Brown's life for a long time to come.

A pager number attached to one of the files led police to Heddi Larae Ille and she answered the page using Michelle Brown's name. The police called her bluff and advised her to turn herself in the next day. She agreed, but then asked for additional time to organize her surrender. The California police issued a warrant for Ille's arrest but Texas authorities beat them to the punch. Ille was arrested in May of 1999 for drug smuggling. As she was still living under Michelle Brown's identity, the arrest was surprisingly also made in Brown's name. Ille was released despite the fact Brown had placed a fraud flag on her driver's license that should have alerted the arresting officers to the broader problem. Brown, however, was not notified of this arrest. In July 1999, Ille was arrested again, this time with drugs, credit cards that had been re-imprinted with Brown's name, and a driver's license with Brown's name and Ille's photograph. She faced 13 criminal charges. "She identified herself as me even … as the police came to her hotel door," said Brown. By September, Michelle Brown's identity thief was convicted of three state felony counts of perjury, grand theft, and possession of stolen property, each carrying a penalty of two years to be served concurrently. While Brown was relieved that Ille was serving prison time, the thief was never convicted of identity theft or impersonation. She was later convicted of possession with intent to distribute 3,000 pounds (1,364 kg) of marijuana in 2000 and sentenced to 73 months in prison.

Michelle Brown's story does not end there. Even after Ille's arrest, Brown continued to fight the association. After a trip to Mexico, she was detained at Los Angeles International Airport's Customs and Immigration. There she spent an hour explaining the situation and the unfortunate events that linked her to Heddi Ille's crimes. Only after customs officials received verification from police detectives that everything Michelle Brown told them was true would they release her. Then, a month after Ille's conviction, the criminal was transferred to the Chicago Federal Prison where she was booked in Michelle Brown's name. This error, Brown was told, would be corrected, but Brown never received proof of this amendment. She still worries about her record and her credit and refuses to leave the country for fear that she'll be held responsible for Heddi Larae Ille's acts.

Brown was forever changed by this ordeal and is afraid the "Michelle Brown" that Ille stole will never return. "No words will ever be strong enough to completely convince others what this period was like—filled with terror, aggravation, unceasing anger, and frustration as I woke every day [since my discovery of the identity fraud in January 1999] with emotionally charged, livid angst," she explained in her written testimony to the Senate Committee. She hopes the government will make changes to allow law enforcement to impose stiffer sentences on identity thieves and better protect potential victims. Then no one will again have to live through what she did at the hands of a remorseless identity thief.

A Step Behind

You don't have to be famous or become famous to be victimized by an identity thief. In 1996, a 23-year-old Vancouver, British Columbia, student found out the hard way how invasive and frustrating this crime can be. Shelby Laidlaw was working her way through college at a gas station, and it was there that someone reached over the counter and stole her wallet and daytimer one morning. She thought she knew who it was, remembering a customer earlier in the day. "There was a sketchy looking guy who had come in and I went to my boss after he left and said if there's anything missing today, that guy stole it," she says. She was so suspicious, she jotted down part of the car's license plate, but in the end it wasn't enough to track the car. Laidlaw reported her wallet stolen to the Royal Canadian Mounted Police (RCMP) dispatch nearby and canceled her cards. She thought it was over, but unfortunately it had only begun.

A month after her wallet was stolen, Shelby received a letter from the Ministry of Small Business and Economic Development outlining her name approval request to start her own business. "I thought it was junk mail at first, but then I pulled it back out of the garbage and showed it to my mom," says Laidlaw. Her mother urged her to call the agency to investigate the business application, and it turned out that someone had submitted the request but told the agent that she would return to pick up the results in person so there was no need to mail them. This clerical error is how Laidlaw discovered someone else was using her name.

The quick-thinking student set up her file so that only one person at the ministry would deal with it to ensure someone stayed on top of the account and that nothing fell through the cracks. When the woman who filed the papers returned to pick up the name approval, police promptly arrested her. She had Laidlaw's driver's license, college identification card, and her St. John's first aid certificate on her at the time of the arrest, and the woman, "R. R.," was charged with using forged documents, impersonation, and possession of stolen property. This alleged identity thief was clever, however; rather than declare, "I'm Shelby Laidlaw here to pick up my documents," she was careful to say, "I'm here to pick up documents for Shelby Laidlaw." Because of this semantic point, there wasn't enough evidence to prosecute her for anything other than possession of stolen property. For the next six months R. R., her lawyer, or both parties missed court dates and the case was adjourned and postponed until R. R. was finally found guilty and sentenced to a one-year conditional sentence, served in the community, and a $35 fine to go to victim services.

This was not, however, the last of Shelby Laidlaw's ordeal. In January of 1997, a man was arrested in New Westminster with her CARE medical card, her Royal Bank client card, and her library card on him. A few months later, a residence search in Langley, British Columbia, turned up more of Laidlaw's identification, along with many other people's. Shortly after this, the Burnaby police called Laidlaw at work, saying she was being summoned to appear in court to face charges of theft under

$5000. Someone using her identification was caught stealing panty hose from a Safeway grocery store, and the arresting security officer let the thief (who fit the description of R. R.) go with a promise to appear. Laidlaw had to get letters from her employer and her school instructors to corroborate her whereabouts on the day of the theft to finally prove her innocence and have the charges cleared. A few months following this, the Surrey police contacted Laidlaw regarding an outstanding fine for riding the sky train without buying a ticket. Despite the birthdate and address on record being different, the ticket was tracked to Shelby Laidlaw and, as before, it was up to her to clear up the mistake. In British Columbia, unpaid tickets prevent residents from renewing their driver's licenses, so Laidlaw had to complete stacks of paperwork before she could drive.

While the fraudulent use of her identity didn't cost her significant sums in the end, it was a horrible and long experience for her. "So that's three cities now and four different case files," says Laidlaw. "I was in court a million times, and spent tons of time on the phone trying to get different people to do different things." There were forms to sign and notarize, and travel time to different jurisdictions. She placed flags on her credit report and for close to two years she requested that her bank check her signature card and ask for identification before completing any transactions. She had to contact victim services and have them run her name to ensure there weren't any outstanding warrants before she crossed the border into the United States for vacations. It's been an exhausting and frustrating experience—one she will never forget. "It cost me hundreds of dollars, but it could have been a lot worse," she says. She acted quickly and kept very thorough records of every phone call, every form, and every detail of each instance and keeps the binder in a safe place even today. She still looks over her shoulder and expects that something else will come up. She shreds everything and is guarded with her personal information. The worst part of it for Laidlaw is that she knows R. R. is still out there, likely scamming someone else. "You know what? In cases like this, crime does pay," the cynic says.

The Case That Rocked the Nation

In November 2002, Southern New York's United States Attorney's Office was thrilled to bring down what authorities were calling the biggest identity theft case in the country's history. Philip Cummings was a help-desk employee at Long Island's Teledata Communications Inc. (TCI), a company that offered banks and other companies access to consumer credit information from three commercial credit history bureaus. TCI gave clients both software and hardware that allowed them to then download credit reports using passwords and subscriber codes. Cummings worked directly with clients so he had privileged access to clients' codes and passwords, which opened the door for him to download unauthorized credit reports for himself. In 2000, Cummings began downloading credit reports from a list of wealthy people given to him by an acquaintance named Linus Baptiste—Baptiste received up to $60 for each credit report he provided and the two split the bounty. Cummings and his conspirator fueled a network exceeding 20 credit card fraudsters who used his information to commit identity theft. Many of these people have pleaded guilty to charges relating to this case. Cummings turned lists of names and addresses into complete credit reports issued in those individual's names, which gave the identity thieves who purchased this information all they needed to steal their victims' money, their identities, or both. Even after Cummings left his job and moved to Georgia, the theft continued. The police believe he returned to New York to download these stolen reports and then later left his accomplice with a stolen TCI laptop computer and instructions about how to use it. When a client changed a password, Cummings simply moved on to another company and password on his list and also gave it to Baptiste.

Over the course of about three years, Cummings and his conspirators stole the information of more than 30,000 people, which led to the loss of what investigators pegged, at the time, to be more than $2.7 million. By 2005, a more accurate number was established that reflected the magnitude of this theft ring: between $50 and $100 million. Many unsuspecting victims lost their life savings and, at the end of the day, were faced with huge lines of credit and other debts. The Grand Rapids, Michigan, branch of the Ford Motor Credit Corp. was one company to have its passwords and codes stolen by Cummings. After 10 months and 15,000 credit reports, Ford questioned bills submitted by credit bureau Experian, which had provided these credit reports, and thus discovered the fraud. By that time, many of Ford's customers had complained (as had many victims at other companies) about being victims of identity theft that ranged from the use of their information to empty bank accounts to strangers operating under their assumed names. As well, Experian discovered the same scam, resulting in thousands of stolen credit reports, had been run against institutions across the country such as Washington Mutual Bank in Florida, Dollar Bank in Cleveland, Ohio, branches of the Washington Mutual Finance Company, Sarah Bush Lincoln Health Center in Illinois, Community Bank of Chaska in Minnesota, and the Medical Bureau in Clearwater, Florida.

In October 2002, an FBI raid on Baptiste's residence turned up computers and stolen credit reports hidden throughout his bedroom. Baptiste then helped authorities turn their attention to ringleader Philip Cummings. Later, Baptiste pleaded guilty to charges of wire fraud after his phone numbers were shown to have called into Equifax's databases to download between 400 and 600 credit reports. With charges including wire fraud against him, Cummings faced up to 30 years in prison and up to $1 million in fines; for conspiracy charges, he faced up to five years in prison and up to $250,000 in fines. Cummings pleaded guilty and, in 2005, was sentenced to 14 years in prison. In response to this sentence, Cummings simply said, "I'm very, very sorry for my conduct in this case. I normally don't get into this kind of trouble."

The FBI laid charges against other individuals believed to be involved in the Cummings case as well. Hakeem Mohammad pleaded guilty to mail fraud and conspiracy for his part in the ring. He was charged after making an address change to a line of credit that had been opened in the names of two Ford Motor Credit victims, and for opening accounts and lines of credit using the name of two additional Ford victims. He was sentenced to 41 months in prison. Data buyer Eniete Ukpong was arrested for using the stolen information to open credit card accounts; he had passed much of the stolen goods acquired with this credit to Ahmet Ulutas to sell overseas. Each pleaded guilty to these offenses in 2004. The bust was significant in both size and scope. It not only drew attention to this crime, it also showed North Americans how vulnerable we all are to the ravages of identity theft. "We believe this is the largest case of identity fraud in U.S. history, with the losses running into the many, many millions," said U.S. Attorney James Comey to reporters. Comey described the crime as "every American's worst financial nightmare multiplied tens of thousands of times."

Our Secrets are Not Safe

The Cummings case proved that even large corporations were susceptible to information theft that led to identity crimes. Data warehouses hold detailed dossiers of information on nearly everyone, often without our knowledge. Files are put together from public records such as court records, property tax files, registration and licensing information, as well as credit reports and consumer demographics. One of the largest data aggregators is ChoicePoint, with about 19 billion records. It collects, stores, and sells information about most American adults. Companies purchasing this information include employers, loan officers, debt collectors, media, law offices, and law enforcement. Citizens can receive a copy of their own files for free from ChoicePoint as well. But in February 2005, ChoicePoint admitted that a Nigerian fraudster named Olatunji Oluwatosin had created 50 phony companies in 2004 and managed to access the data warehouser's information—to the tune of about 145,000 files. The Southern California High Tech Task Force's Lt. Robert Costa believed an accurate count would be much higher: 500,000 files. Using fake letterhead for fabricated debt collection, insurance, and check-cashing businesses, Oluwatosin fax ordered these dossiers for $150 per batch from a Hollywood, California, copy shop. These files were filled with individuals' birthdates, Social

Security numbers, and other vital information that enabled Oluwatosin to launch successful and simple identity theft.

A ChoicePoint employee noticed something unusual and became suspicious about one of Oluwatosin's applications for information so the authorities were called in to help. When Oluwatosin was arrested at the copy shop, he had three credit cards and five cell phones on him, all registered under different names. Although he pleaded no contest to charges of felony identity theft and was sentenced to 16 months in prison, police know others must have been a part of this scheme—there have been more than 750 reported cases of identity theft or attempted fraud linked to this theft. Oluwatosin, however, is staying mum about the existence of accomplices.

For its part, ChoicePoint reached out to help people affected by this breach, including offering free credit monitoring for victims for a year. But ChoicePoint is paying the price for a very public security disaster. Not only did its stock plummet, victims filed at least three class-action law suits against the data broker, including one accusing ChoicePoint of concealing information and waiting to release the news of the breach until executives could sell shares. ChoicePoint CEO Derek Smith stated in prepared testimony before the House Energy and Commerce Committee, "The security breach has caused us to go through some serious soul searching." That soul searching might well have been more effective earlier, in 2001, when a similar breach occurred. Because this occurred before the California law compelling companies to report information breaches was passed, ChoicePoint did not make that incident known at the time.

About two weeks after the ChoicePoint breach was made public, Bank of America released details of its own serious security breach, as required by California law. The organization had lost several backup tapes that held the information for 1.2 million federal employees' credit card accounts. The files, which were not encrypted, were apparently flown to the data center but never arrived. Bank officials desperately searched for the missing tapes, even calling in the Secret Service to help. For a month, investigators tried to find the tapes, but potential victims were kept in the dark. The bank watched over accounts to make sure there wasn't unusual activity, but nothing was detected. In February 2005, Bank of America disclosed the situation and assured clients that it had changed procedures to ensure this would never happen again. It also promised free credit reports and fraud monitoring for affected customers. While Bank of America officials contend that the information was never used by identity thieves, the incident left people shocked and enraged by how their information had been handled. Jim Stickley, of threat-management company TraceSecurity, is paid to essentially break into banks to test their security weaknesses. He was stunned by Bank of America's negligence. In an interview with *Fortune* magazine, Stickley made this assessment: "Everything you want to protect is on those tapes. If they're not encrypted, strike No. 1. Then they're using commercial carriers to transfer the tapes, and they're like, 'Everybody does that.' But that's not the case. It's not like it's a surprise that stuff can be stolen from commercial airlines. I think there are several bad choices they made ... that could have been avoided." Not to be outdone, CitiFinancial packaged up tapes in May 2005 filled with customers' names, addresses, Social Security numbers, and loan-payment records. It was to be shipped from New Jersey to Texas, but the boxes never arrived. This left 3.9 million customers wondering where the boxes ended up and who had access to this sensitive data.

Yet another data broker, LexisNexis, found itself in a similar predicament in March 2005. The broker had acquired two databases as part of a $775 million purchase of Seisint Inc., an information compiler in Florida. These entities were to be brought into LexisNexis' U.S. Risk Management business. The security breach was related to those newly acquired business units. The company announced that identity thieves may have stolen sensitive data such as names, Social Security numbers, driver's license numbers, and addresses (but not the credit histories, financial data, or medical records) of about 32,000 people. That number was soon expanded to about 310,000. LexisNexis contacted clients and offered affected customers account and credit report monitoring to safeguard them against identity theft and fraud. Internally, LexisNexis has tightened security procedures and added resources to the area of consumer privacy in order to avoid a similar breach.

While these incidents left consumers shocked and angry, the security breach at Atlanta-based CardSystems Solutions Inc. left people stunned and outraged. This private company processes about $15 billion in credit card transactions each year with credit card providers that include MasterCard, Visa, American Express, and Discover. Against protocol, this company kept 40 million credit card numbers (including the secret code numbers found on the back of the cards) in its system— reportedly for research. Skilled hackers broke into the system in May 2005 and relieved CardSystems of this information, leaving a staggering 40 million people at risk of identity theft. This incident marked the largest data breach in American history. About 14 million of these cards were MasterCard-branded credit cards, while about 22 million were Visa credit cards. CardSystems has since beefed up security to keep our information safe, but that's little comfort to potential victims or their credit card companies. In July 2005, Visa USA Inc. severed its relationship with CardSystems, claiming that the company had not corrected the problems that caused the breach in the first place and it didn't believe CardSystems could correct the problem at that time. Visa did concede that CardSystem had made some changes to help protect clients, but Visa decided these weren't adequate to guarantee protection for its cardholders.

North of the border, the Canadian Imperial Bank of Canada (CIBC) also put clients at risk by mishandling sensitive information. For three years, bank personnel erroneously and continually faxed personal information about hundreds of its clients to a scrap yard in West Virginia. Branches across Canada sent faxes to what they believed to be the bank's central faxing unit. It wasn't. Beginning in 2001, scrap yard operator Wade Peer received scads of internal fund transfer request forms for retirement savings plans and income funds over his fax line, all of which displayed Social Insurance numbers, addresses, account data, and addresses. Peer could easily see the delicate nature of the faxes and tried to shred as many as he could, but the volume was overwhelming. "Had I been a bad guy, I could have got credit cards in their name, I could have assumed their identity. I could have transferred money out of their bank accounts and they'd never know that it happened," Peer told *CTV News*. Peer says he contacted the CIBC about the mistake, but he continued to receive the forms for years. He even contacted some of the extremely unhappy customers whose information was sent to him to try to motivate CIBC to make the situation right. The bank, however, believed the problem was remedied in 2002 and was distressed to hear faxes were still arriving at the scrap yard. Wade Peer claimed the flow of faxes caused him to have to shut down a new business venture and he filed a lawsuit against the CIBC. The Office of the Superintendent of Financial Institutions (OSFI) continued to investigate the situation in 2005. Hundreds of CIBC clients, in the meantime, can only thank their lucky stars that Wade Peer remained an honest man and didn't use the information he received.

Credit reporting companies are not immune from the stink of security breaches. In

2004, one of Canada's major agencies, Equifax-Canada, announced it had suffered a security breach. Criminals duped the company out of files containing bank account numbers, credit histories, and addresses. Equifax quickly informed the 1,400 people at risk after the breach and offered each a free subscription to a service that alerts people if someone accesses their files. While a terrible event, vice-president Joel Heft said in a Canadian Broadcasting Corporation (CBC) interview that it could have been much worse: "While it's a large number, it's 1,400 out of our data base of 30 million, and it's relatively minor compared to some of the data spills we've heard of over time." Those 1,400 potential victims likely disagree with this dismissal.

Thief in the Family

Families are about people who are there for us, no matter what. Or at least that's how it's supposed to be. But in nine percent of all identity theft cases, the thief is flesh and blood—that translates to about 900,000 cases. Whether due to gambling or money troubles, drug problems, or just bad blood between kin, these all-in-the-family culprits inflict additional shock and pain on victims. Abigail Kelly was close to her younger sister, Delia, and didn't think twice when her sister asked her to be a beneficiary of her life insurance policy. Of course, to do so, she would need Abigail's Social Security number—which Abigail provided without question.

A while later, Abigail was looking for a new home to rent and conducted a routine credit check to kick off the process. What wasn't routine was the warrant issued for her arrest in Maine for an unpaid bill. Abigail did some digging and found a phone number issued in her name along with bank credit. The worst of it was the culprit was her own sister. Delia had bad credit, so she just used her sister's good name to get what she needed. The police in Maine and the FBI wouldn't help Abigail. Her only recourse was to take her own sister to civil court in

California where she charged she had not only been a financial victim, but she had also lost a job after an employer ran a background check that turned up the warrant. The ruling was in Abigail's favor, and she was awarded $50,000 for distress, lost income, and the damage done to her credit. But Delia, living across the country, felt no obligation to honor the judgment. Abigail went through the process again in Maine and won, and Delia grudgingly agreed to pay the restitution. The ordeal tore the family apart and Abigail lost a sister. "You want to go in there—like the Social Security number is a chip—and just take it out of their head," Abigail Kelly told CBS news.

Stealing Homes

It's hard to imagine someone stealing a house, but it happens every day across the continent. In some cases, victims can have a home sold out from under them. And it's relatively easy for crafty identity thieves to do. In many cases,

it's as simple as forging signatures on a purchase agreement and filing the proper documents, albeit forged, with the land titles office.
Then a criminal walks away with your house,
no questions asked, and is free to take out a
bogus mortgage and pocket the money. In one
case highlighted on the popular Canadian news
program *W-FIVE*, a con man invented a debt
against a homeowner and registered a false lien
on a house. By forging the real owner's, Ramin
Dehmoubed's, signature on a document offering his house as payment of that debt, the thief
was able to essentially steal the house from the
unsuspecting family. The Dehmoubeds had no
idea anything was amiss until one day a for sale
sign appeared on their front lawn. Dehmoubed
promptly called the police who confronted the
suspect, Gideon Augier, and ordered that he
produce proof of this phony debt or he would
be charged. He couldn't, so he was charged with
fraud. It took Dehmoubed four years in court
and thousands of hours and dollars to finally

get his home back. Augier, who had eight fraud convictions dating back to the mid-1980s, was sentenced to 30 days in prison to be served on the weekends and $15,000 restitution to his victim. None of that money was ever paid. "I just can't believe something like that could happen. You buy the house and it's yours, but two years later you find out there's a lien on the house and it's for sale," Dehmoubed told *W-FIVE*. This crime can happen to anyone, and in many cases the victims are chosen completely at random— simply by driving through posh neighborhoods looking for homes to target.

In some other cases of mortgage fraud, thieves file a transfer of ownership paper, and because no one at the land titles office thinks to cross reference the signature, the transfer goes through. This happened to Ontario's Jennifer Fiddian-Green. She was contacted about properties in her name that she knew nothing about and was informed that she owed about $500,000 in payments. As a forensic accountant,

Fiddian-Green dove into the case and uncov-
ered some disturbing information. There were
photocopies of identity documents bearing her
name, date of birth, and Social Insurance number—but with someone else's photograph. She
also received copies of the property titles and
contacted the person who sold the properties.
Through the seller, she was able to turn authorities on to two men who had put the deal through
for the phony Fiddian-Green. Charges were laid
in the case but there wasn't enough evidence to
prove the men were knowingly acting on behalf
of someone fraudulently claiming to be Jennifer Fiddian-Green—this despite the fact that
one of the men was already appearing in court
on charges of stealing someone's identity to acquire mortgage money.

This fraud is being committed more and
more across Canada, but police are having
trouble investigating and prosecuting the offense. Banks in Canada are not required to
report instances of mortgage fraud to police.

Because banks are ultimately the victims if they lose the mortgage money once a case is prosecuted, police require cooperation in order to make cases against the thieves. Without a cooperative victim, police are stymied. In the United States, however, mortgage fraud is more openly discussed, and banks partner with law enforcement to help each other fight this growing crime. National conventions and seminars are held across the country to combat this problem and feature experts who speak about the situation. At one such convention, the Assistant Director of the Criminal Investigation Division of the FBI, Chris Swecker, said, "It wouldn't take an amazing grasp of the obvious to state we have a problem. It has the potential to impact our financial systems, our economy." He said mortgage fraud had ballooned five-fold between 2000 and 2004, with cases growing from 4,000 to 17,000, and aggressive action needed to be taken to slow its advance. Laws need to allow for serious sentences for offenders to provide deterrents because mortgage fraud is a relatively low-risk, lucrative crime. Without laws that require banks to report cases, mortgage fraudsters will continue to take over home owners' names to steal their houses or to take out mortgages in their names.

CHAPTER 4

Fighting Identity Theft

There are countless organizations across North America that are dedicated to helping protect consumers against fraud and who can offer assistance in the event that identity crimes are committed against them.

PhoneBusters

In Canada, one key organization to contact regarding identity theft is PhoneBusters, the

Canadian Anti-fraud Call Centre. The Ontario Provincial Police, the Canadian Competition Bureau, and the RCMP established this organization in 1993 to prosecute deceptive telemarketers in Ontario and Quebec. It was streamlined in 2001 to respond to the growth and spread of identity theft. "We decided to central-source identity theft into one location because the U.S. had such a problem and nobody really knew how big a problem it was here," says Staff Sergeant Barry Elliot. Now PhoneBusters also works side-by-side with United States agencies, facilitating extradition in fraud cases that cross borders.

Since its inception, PhoneBusters has closely studied this type of crime from coast to coast—its changing trends and patterns, and how best to fight it from a consumer and a law enforcement standpoint. Along the way, this agency has collected data that serves to alert the public to the seriousness of the problem of identity theft in this country; one of the

organization's major mandates is public awareness about identity theft and what you can do
to avoid becoming a victim. PhoneBusters' research also aids police department task forces
to better understand how the crime is perpetrated, by whom, and how to investigate cases
as well as apprehend and prosecute the offenders more effectively.

The PhoneBusters call center receives
about 15,000 complaints of identity theft each
year, but the actual number of victims is likely
far higher. Much of the identity theft involving
credit cards is reported to financial institutions
but not to the police or PhoneBusters. These
cases aren't factored into the statistics, demographics, or the data compiled and disseminated by the organization. In many situations,
victims are embarrassed about what has happened and their perceived role in allowing it to
happen. They don't want to report the theft, so
these cases remain under-represented.

Identity Theft Resource Center

The American nonprofit organization, Identity Theft Resource Center (ITRC), has been battling the scourge that is identity theft since Linda and Jay Foley founded it in 1999. Identity theft hits close to home for this husband and wife team. In 1997, Linda's employer used her personal information to acquire a credit card and a cell phone. Foley found that there was little information available about or support for victims of identity theft at that time, and she recognized the need for a program devoted to this complicated crime. Today, the Identity Theft Resource Center, based in San Diego, California, is an important provider of assistance to and service for victims of identity theft. It received the 2004 Department of Justice National Crime Victims Service Award for its efforts in this area.

ITRC is a valuable resource for advice and information for victims, consumers, businesses, and law enforcement, and it welcomed more than a million visitors to the organization's web site in 2004. The detailed and thorough web site is often all victims need to navigate their course through reporting the crime and reclaiming their identity. "Other people want a more hands-on approach, so we sit there and guide them through the process," says co-executive director Linda Foley. She is happy to simplify the process, laying out the steps to take and the order in which to take them. In some complicated cases, she also puts victims in touch with investigators to help them get the information they need for their case. ITRC's role varies from case to case: sometimes it involves providing translators to help people communicate with credit bureaus and collection agencies; sometimes it's a matter of a few phone calls to calm victims and get them started on the right path.

By making information about the crime and protection strategies for consumers readily available, the ITRC hopes to slow the runaway train of identity theft. It's a long process, however, and Foley and her full-time paid team of about six, along with roughly 100 amazing volunteers nationwide, are working hard to achieve this goal.

Federal Trade Commission

The Federal Trade Commission (FTC) is an independent government agency that was established in 1914. The FTC was created to set up and guarantee fair trade in the country's economy. With its dedication to American business and consumers, it was drawn into the identity theft whirlwind as a major player right from the start. As such, victims of identity theft file their complaints with the FTC, which operates a database of cases available to law enforcement to facilitate their investigation of crimes nationwide. The information gathered also helps the FTC identify the problems victims face so that changes can possibly be made to alleviate those challenges in the future.

In 1999, the FTC was named the central storehouse for identity theft complaints after the Identity Theft and Assumption Deterrence Act passed the year before. The toll-free hotline allows victims to report the theft and receive advice. The FTC stores more than 815,000 complaints. Here, people can search victim and/ or suspect data from anywhere in the United States.

Not only does the Federal Trade Commission collect information, it also provides a great deal of information about identity theft in general, such as prevention tips, what to do if you are a victim, the laws surrounding identity theft cases, and an update of the latest scams that Americans should watch for. From understanding the crime to recovering from it, the FTC's detailed resources help victims at a confusing and stressful time.

National Banking Associations

Both Canada and the United States have well-established Bankers Associations to represent financial institutions and their customers. The

American Bankers Association in Washington, DC, has been operating since 1875 and now acts on behalf of more than 2,400 banks of all sizes—trust companies, savings banks and associations, and community, regional, and money center banks. The Canadian Bankers Association, established in 1891, has long represented banks across the country and represents most of Canada's chartered banks, with 64 members.

The associations aim to keep the banking industry strong and profitable, which requires acting to prevent the financial fraud perpetrated through identity theft. They have partnered with businesses, consumer groups, and law enforcement on the front lines to increase security and prevent fraud in banking. Such steps as requiring that printed receipts for debit and credit cards conceal a card's expiration date or a portion of the card's number creates roadblocks for identity thieves. Banks and credit card providers are working with consumers to rectify false charges and accounts; they limit the amount of fraudulent charges for which victims are responsible to $50. These service providers also work to educate communities and legislators about these issues to determine the most effective solutions—regulatory and otherwise—to the enormous problem of identity theft and bank fraud.

Law Enforcement

Identity theft is a crime that strikes victims everywhere. Most city police departments receive complaints about one aspect of identity theft or another, and some have created specialized units within their departments to deal with these crimes. From British Columbia to Florida, professionals are educating the public about the threat of identity theft and how to protect its members against it. They also educate officers about diverse, high-tech methods to track crooks (including use of the Internet) to better tackle this crime. Across the continent, governments and policing agencies are joining together to form strong, citywide or statewide task forces and fraud squads to bring down identity thieves. In cities that include Detroit, Chicago, Memphis, and Mobile, successful identity theft task forces are working side-by-side with all levels of law enforcement and government, along with employees from affected retailers, to combat the crime's spread. The Chicago Metro Identity Theft Task Force, for example, has enjoyed great success in its efforts to stamp out identity theft. Between 2003 and May 2005, it made 39 arrests that resulted in 11 indictments and 19 prosecutions. The introduction or expansion of working groups and task forces in

A SPRINGBOARD TO OTHER TYPES OF CRIME

"United States and Canadian law enforcement agencies are seeing a growing trend in both countries towards greater use of identity theft as a means of furthering or facilitating other types of crime, from fraud to organized crime to terrorism."

Source: "Public Advisory: Special Report for Consumers on Identity Theft" prepared by the Department of the Solicitor General of Canada and the U.S. Department of Justice areas like Tampa, San Diego, and Philadelphia also serve to target these crimes and criminals.

The Sacramento Valley Hi-Tech Crimes Task Force's Identity Theft Task Force consists of nine detectives, one sergeant, and an identity theft prosecutor who focus entirely on the problem of identity theft. Despite this dedication, caseloads are overwhelming, and the team is forced to consider the amount of loss, the nature of leads on suspects, and the number of victims to prioritize cases. This means not all cases are reviewed immediately, which leaves victims frustrated and thieves free to prosper from their crimes.

The Identity Theft Task Force (ITTF) in Vancouver, British Columbia, was established in 2005 to track down suspects who commit mail theft, identity theft, and crimes committed in an effort to collect personal and financial information (by breaking into offices to steal files or stealing material from cars or mailboxes). As part of its mandate, the ITTF has initiated an intelligence databank and also provides training to patrol officers. This task force includes a liaison between financial institutions, insurance companies, retail investigators, and other businesses to facilitate the pooling of resources to fight identity theft.

Federal, state, and municipal law enforcement and prosecutors united in the Las Vegas Valley in 2004 to battle the growing problem of financial and identity theft in the area. SWIFT (Southwestern Identity Theft and Fraud Task Force) is made up of members of the U.S. Secret Service, police departments from Las Vegas and surrounding areas, the U.S. Attorney's Office and the Clark County District Attorney's Office, and the U.S. Postal Inspection Service. Together, they primarily investigate complicated fraud and identity theft cases perpetrated by criminal organizations.

The Federal Bureau of Investigation

For decades, the FBI has tackled some of the

toughest crimes—racketeering, terrorist attacks, corruption in public office, and the like. The FBI is now setting its sights on an equally challenging endeavor by supporting and actively participating in many efforts to fight identity theft. In the first half of 2005, the FBI had more than 1,600 identity cases pending across all of its programs: this crime, then, is receiving considerable attention. The FBI partners with various task forces across the country, along with agencies such as the FTC, to bring down major identity-theft criminals and organizations. The FBI also sponsors initiatives that include a national Identity Theft Working Group that enables law enforcement, federal regulatory officials, and members of the financial services industry to meet regularly to discuss identity theft in the hopes of identifying and initiating long-term solutions.

The Internet Fraud Complaint Center (IFCC) was a joint project between the FBI and the National White Collar Crime Center.

It was established in 2000 in response to the rise in fraud committed through the Internet, and it gives victims a simple means to report the crime. It also helps law enforcement identify and track trends, and it alerts authorities to new scams and violations that harness the Internet. In 2003, the IFCC was renamed the Internet Crime Complaint Center to encompass all crimes perpetrated on the Internet. Because computers and the Internet are the tools for many identity thieves, this Center is crucial to fighting identity theft. In only five years, it has received more than 100,000 complaints related to identity theft, and in 2004, the Center averaged more than 17,000 consumer complaints each month.

Reporting Economic Crime Online

Reporting Economic Crime Online (RECOL) is an RCMP-run resource. This Canadian web-based initiative brings together international, federal, and provincial law enforcement, along with regulators and private organizations that have legitimate interests in receiving copies of economic crime complaints, including those involving identity theft. RECOL also offers victims guidance through the investigation and reporting process along with consumer education about awareness and prevention. RECOL shares data about fraud trends, economic crimes, and the reports that are entered by victims with organizations and law enforcement in an attempt to combat this crime.

The Privacy Rights Clearinghouse

One major debate embroiled in the proliferation of identity theft is the right to privacy and the protection of that privacy. The Privacy Rights Clearinghouse (PRC) is a nonprofit organization that strives to provide consumer information and acts as an advocate for consumer rights. Since 1992, this California organization has raised awareness about personal privacy issues and has protected citizens across the country through seminars, information campaigns, and its consumer hotline, where people can lodge complaints of privacy abuses or request specific information.

The PRC has been very interested in identity theft; indeed, it is the topic about which it is contacted most often. It receives between 60 and 100 phone calls and e-mails each week on the subject. The topics of these contacts vary from queries about companies shredding (or not shredding) materials, to "data miners" gaining access and misappropriating consumer information, to fingerprinting as a means to protect consumers and verify identities. The PRC also offers guidance with fact sheets about organizing a case and advice and contacts, if consumers find they are victims of identity theft.

Credit Bureaus

Credit reporting is a critical part of life around the world—it allows people to make purchases by enabling retailers and institutions to quickly access personal information. These files, which are constantly changed and updated, must be protected and yet accessible to businesses that require information. We look to credit bureaus to give organizations an accurate portrait of our financial situation and capabilities, and thus ensure we can get the car loan, home mortgage, or line of credit we can afford. When identity theft occurs, the neglect of payment and debt accumulation reflects on our good names and is captured on our credit reports.

The credit bureaus have made prevention of identity theft a part of daily business by implementing fraud departments and other measures to help clear unwarranted credit black marks from a victim's report. "Credit bureaus here do a pretty good job weeding through the thousands of false applications that are attempted … through the system and stopping them from being approved," says Barry Elliot of PhoneBusters. But fraudulent applications still sneak through and credit bureaus are the first places victims should call when they discover a fraud, so alerts can be issued on their credit reports. Victims need to contact only one of the three credit bureaus in the United States and two in Canada: the company will then call the other bureau or bureaus and instruct them to place an alert on their files as well.

Equifax, Experian, and TransUnion in the United States, and Equifax Canada and Trans-Union Canada north of the border, all have fraud departments trained to handle cases of identity theft. They also offer credit report monitoring as a form of insurance so victims can keep a close watch on their credit and be notified immediately in the event of activity. Costs for this service vary depending on the company and country, but many victims have opted for constant monitoring to prevent the nightmare from happening again.

Identity Theft Assistance Center

The Financial Services Roundtable is an association of large banks in the United States that represents institutions responsible for about 70 percent of the American economy's financial transactions. In May 2004, this association launched a pilot program for member corporations called the Identity Theft Assistance Center (ITAC). The ITAC allows information about identity theft cases to reach credit card companies, financial institutions, and law enforcement all with one call. The ITAC places fraud alerts on victims' files at credit bureaus and helps victims understand their credit reports. Consumers, however, don't contact the center directly. Instead, they meet with an ombudsman at their bank to discuss what should be done, and then the bank employee contacts the assistance center with case information.

The Identity Theft Assistance Center collects information from numerous sources, including credit bureau reports and consumers, and shares this information with law enforcement and the FTC to help find and prosecute identity thieves. This center is just one of the steps the financial services industry has implemented to fight identity theft, and representatives are optimistic it will help reduce the heavy financial and emotional impact of the identity theft epidemic.

CHAPTER 5

The History

Only 20 years ago, the term "identity theft" was virtually unheard of. How could someone steal who you are? The only kind of theft people fretted about was all but prevented by locking doors. That was then. The evolution of identity theft has been swift over the past few decades, keeping pace with the advancements in technology that make the scam easier. Only since the late 1990s has identity theft become a recognizable phrase in the North American lexicon, and it has since exploded to become a dreaded crime affecting people in all regions and walks of life.

Impersonation has figured throughout history as a simple way to separate people from their money, but the con wasn't referred to specifically as "identity theft." For hundreds of years, people have claimed to be someone they are not in order to get money or social status or avoid responsibility for some misdeed committed under another name. In the 1100s and 1200s, the deaths of rulers like the Holy Roman Emperor Frederick Barbarossa, Baldwin of Antioch, and Frederick II Hohenstaufen brought forth a rush of imposters claiming to be the rulers or their descendents. In Russia, the often mysterious deaths of royalty invited imposters to claim to be the son of Ivan the Terrible or the lost Anastasia. This type of con continued for centuries—time and again a poor man or woman posed as someone else to escape his or her station in life. Archibald Belaney even posed as a member of a different race, and under the name of Grey Owl he enjoyed the success and attention that came with three bestselling books about life as an Indian. More recently, Christopher Rocancourt duped the American elite into believing he was a French Rockefeller, the son of Sophia Loren, or the nephew to Oscar de la Renta and Dino De Laurentis. He was a boxing champion and a venture capitalist and a prince, depending on who he was talking with at the time and which persona best suited his plans. After establishing himself, Rocancourt drew his wealthy "friends" into investment schemes and walked away with millions.

One of the most famous impersonators and con artists was Frank Abagnale Jr., who wrote *Catch Me if You Can*, which inspired the smash movie in 2003. In the 1960s, at the tender age of 16, Abagnale began taking on false identities that were backed up with phony identification documents so he could cash bad checks. He set up accounts in different names, ordered checks, and then overdrew the account before disappearing. Early on, he opened an account with $100 and the new accounts clerk gave him temporary checks for the account and told him he would receive printed checks and deposit slips in the mail. She told him that if he needed to make deposits, he could use one of the blank slips sitting in the lobby and write his account number on it. Abagnale took a stack of slips and plotted. In an interview in 2000, Abagnale told Norman Swan about the results: "I bought some magnetic ink, the ink that banks use to encode numbers on checks, and I encoded the account number that the bank had assigned me the day before onto the blanks. I then went back to the bank and put the stack onto the shelf in the bank, and everyone who came in put their check right in my bank account." This scheme earned the young man $40,000 and initiated a gifted con man.

He proceeded to defraud banks, airlines,

hotels, and other businesses in a way and on a scale that had never before been seen in the United States. Abagnale used his charming personality (paired with the research he did on various professions and processes) to imperson-ate Pan Am airline pilots in order to cash bogus income checks and travel from place to place throughout the world for free. Abagnale also fell into posing as a doctor in Georgia, a lawyer in Louisiana (with impressive fake transcripts and a degree from Harvard Law School), a sociology professor in Utah, and a bank security guard collecting deposits in Massachusetts—all while continuing to cash bad checks in other names totaling more than $2.5 million.

Frank Abagnale knew his lifestyle couldn't last. He had committed fraud in 26 countries over the course of 5 years. "I always knew I'd get caught. Though the law sometimes sleeps, it never dies," he has said. And catch up with him the law did: he was arrested in France at the age of 21. He spent 5 years in prison, first in France and then Sweden, before being extradited to the United States where he received a 12-year sentence. He was granted early release in return for helping the FBI counter fraud and counterfeiting, which he did for free to pay back his debt to society. After working odd jobs that didn't pay well or last long, he decided to make his knowledge work for him. He began taking paid speaking engagements from the FBI and law enforcement agencies to discuss the criminal mind and his experiences.

As the years passed, Frank Abagnale's expertise was in high demand by major corporations across the country looking to save themselves millions of dollars in fraud costs. He became known as one of the leading experts on document fraud, check swindling, and forgery. Today, Abagnale has a successful consultant business through which he has counseled 14,000 institutions, law enforcement agencies, and corporations, a huge percentage of which were Fortune 500 companies. With the growing availability of technology, Frank Abagnale recognized early on the enormous potential of identity crime's impact on people and the economy. "The crime of the future will be identity theft, and we're already starting to see where people assume other people's identit[ies] because they are able to get bits and pieces of information about that individual—their bank account, their Social Security or health card number," Abagnale told Swan. He advises people to be cautious of the Internet and to protect themselves by being careful of what information they are leaving in cyberspace.

While Frank Abagnale was a famous impersonator and fraud artist, other notorious figures became infamous identity thieves at a time when the crime was just hitting the headlines. While awaiting his trial, one high-profile identity thief—James Rinaldo Jackson, who we discussed in the introduction—met another identity thief by the name of Abraham Abdallah. Jackson may have stunned authorities and made waves in certain circles, but Abdallah seemed to become the face of identity theft and its evolution. It seemed unthinkable that a high school dropout working as a bus boy in New York City could defraud more than 200 of *Forbes* magazine's "400 Richest People in America." In fact, he had a very well-worn copy of that October 2000 publication in his vehicle when he was arrested. Abdallah had jotted notes beside articles about the wealthiest people in the country and the world citing their account numbers, phone numbers, and the names of key financial advisers he needed to complete his thefts. More incredible was that he covered his tracks by using web-enabled cell phones and virtual voice mail. In addition, he routed his computer activity through the Brooklyn Public Library's computers, which enabled him to pull off one of the greatest fraud sprees in the country. His targets ranged from CNN founder Ted Turner, home improvement maven Martha Stewart, and talk show tycoon Oprah Winfrey.

Abdallah first obtained a victim's Social Security number. Armed with this and some smooth talking, he could uncover other important data like banking information, passwords, addresses, and phone numbers. To make his scams easier on himself, he contacted a private investigator (PI) and claimed to be from Sprint. He wanted to hire the detective to do background checks, and all he needed was a copy of his license and his rates. The PI faxed everything over, and Abdallah used this information to open an account with a database company that catered to private investigators. For only $300 a month, he could now get all the Social Security numbers he wanted. From there, he also received credit reports from the major agencies by sending letters on counterfeit bank stationary.

Abdallah was primed with information and was now ready to put it to work. This time, he was going after the big fish and expected big gains. "I figured for the same work and preparation required to do $1 million or $1.6 million,

I could do $100 million. So why bother with the small money?" he told Mike Boal in a 2004 interview with *Playboy* magazine. He attempted a few transactions that did not go through, including depositing a $10 million check in the name of financier George Soros. The activity sent up flags, and the bank that received it carefully examined the check. It didn't clear, and the police and Secret Service were called. Abdallah wasn't discouraged: he had more identities to steal. Soon he took on the name of Goldman Sachs' chairman Hank Paulson, Microsoft billionaire Paul Allen, Monster.com owner Andrew McKelvey, and many other corporate heavy hitters. Abdallah was able to access and link accounts and then attempt to transfer $200 million in Monster.com stock to one account he had set up, and $38 million from Intel's Gordon Moore into another account. He established accounts across the country and around the world to keep transferring, hiding, and withdrawing money, and he relied on several notebooks he carried to keep all of his scams straight.

The brilliant identity thief was depressed and under stress—loving the highs of the con but falling to lows that were only raised by another theft. "I couldn't stop. I wanted to stop but I couldn't. I wanted to be a success so bad. I wanted to do this on my own," he told Mike Boal. For six months, Abdallah stayed a step ahead of the authorities and never stopped cloning identities and commandeering bank accounts. He was finally caught as a result of using credit cards bearing the names of his victims. His objective? To order computer equipment necessary to create counterfeit documents. The police had been tracking the credit card use and arrested Abdallah when he went to pick up a new hard drive.

In March 2001, the 32-year-old identity thief pleaded guilty to 12 counts of felony fraud covering wire, mail, and credit card fraud, as well as identity theft and conspiracy.

Authorities guessed that Abdallah's crimes garnered more than $80 million, but some estimated his earnings exceeded $260 million in January 2001. The idea that people like former Disney CEO Michael Eisner and presidential candidate Ross Perot could be victimized sent a chill down Americans' backs. With all their security and aides, these individuals were still vulnerable to identity theft. What chance did the common folk have?

Before these cases came to light in 2001, identity theft was a shocking event. In 1993, a California woman lost her identity at her doctor's office, courtesy of a shady receptionist when identity theft was on the rise. The receptionist took Adelaide Andrews' information and applied for credit reports at four different agencies. The agency supplied file information but the credit applications were denied. This information stayed on Andrews' file and she discovered the fraud two years later. When she tried to take action against the credit agency, she met resistance. Judge John T. Noonan came to this conclusion: "It is quintessentially a job for the jury to decide whether identity theft has been common enough for it to be reasonable for a credit reporting agency to disclose credit information merely because a last name matches a social security number on file." The courts finally heard the case in 2001, and the judge decided that even though Andrews hadn't known about the fraud at the time of its occurrence, the statute of limitations had run out and wouldn't be extended.

Despite the loss, the case and the judge demonstrated that little was known about identity theft or how to deal with it in the early 1990s. This is not to say that identity theft wasn't happening. It certainly was, but it took more effort and more time for thieves to gather information. Much early identity theft occurred only after the theft of physical documents that contained critical information: credit card receipts, bank statements, and government documents.

At the time, the introduction of direct-mail pre-approved credit enticements served to grease the wheels of budding identity thieves. Early on, cases of identity theft occurred on a much smaller scale, with fewer losses attached to them than North Americans would come to experience at the turn of the century.

Identity Theft Evolves with Technology

Through the 1990s, computer technology began to flourish and businesses began to move their information from paper files in cabinets to electronic files on computers. The Internet became an absolute necessity in business and in personal lives, both as a source of information and as a part of daily routines. North Americans quickly grew to rely on e-mail accounts and Internet access, and they enjoyed the convenience of shopping and ordering products—from cars to groceries—online. In short order, businesses came to rely on the convenience of using the Internet to send information instantly anywhere in the world—with a touch of a key or the click of a mouse. We thought nothing of companies sending information in this manner, even when that information served to represent our financial selves. We felt safe. We trusted that security was in place, and that it was not only appropriate but impenetrable.

Then something started to happen. The system didn't manage to protect us, and we didn't fully comprehend why this was the case or how to remedy the failures. As the 1990s raced toward the 21st century, North Americans began to be more nervous about the security of information on hard drives and its delivery over the Internet. Whispers about breaches and people—a strange breed called hackers—who could bypass these security measures began to circulate. Suddenly our privacy was at stake, and it seemed as though there was no turning back. By 1998, the naive bliss had evaporated and the truth was realized: criminals, too, had adapted their lives and their habits to the Internet, and they were using advancing technology and the new computer culture (both in business and in people's homes) to make victims by using the information available in cyberspace.

Identity theft has grown exponentially with the Internet. While identity thieves committed theft before by stealing mail and hardcopy files, the computer age opened up a whole new world for them. Not only was information floating out there—virtually—for picking, now criminals could take advantage of technology that made peripherals like quality printers and scanners readily available. Only a decade or two ago, criminals required specialized equipment that cost a great deal of money to acquire, and expertise to use properly, to create documents and other necessities to perpetrate identity theft scams. Now a basic laser printer combined with graphic design software is all that's needed to achieve equivalent results. Moreover, for a small fee criminals can opt to order these forged documents online with ease and convenience, 24 hours a day. Today's Internet further allows identity thieves and cyber-criminals to make transaction after transaction online and gives them access to data banks filled with sensitive information.

How could this happen? And how could it happen here? A 2005 report by The Aite Group suggests that North America, and the United States in particular, is perilously prone to identity theft because of all the consumer information stored within data banks operated by credit agencies and information brokers. "The biggest challenge financial institutions face is the regulatory and business pressure to rely on commercially available data to identify their customers and, at the same time, the extreme vulnerability of those sets of data," says Aite Group's research director, Gwenn Bézard, in a 2005 interview with Maria Santos of *Wall Street & Technology* magazine. Bézard continues: "To reduce the current level of identity theft, financial institutions need to shift the ID verification paradigm—rely less on credit bureaus and information brokers, and rely more on third parties who do not trade consumer data and whose core business is fraud management and ID verification." But this awareness and foresight came with a very steep price: the explosion of identity crime enabled by information stolen from these data banks and used to take over victims' identities.

As computer technology grew and improved, it seemed to invite a greater number of thieves to vie for information on the Internet. However, the most dramatic increase was seen in monetary losses. According to a 2000 report titled *Identity Theft: Authentication as a Solution*, between 1995 and 1997, when Internet usage was beginning to really boom, financial losses from identity theft went from $442 million to $745 million. Consumer calls to the fraud victim assistance department of credit reporting agency TransUnion also soared. In 1992, it received about 35,235 inquiries; in 1997, it fielded 522,922 queries. "The Internet takes the shadowy form of the identity thief and provides him or her [with] the shelter of its anonymity and the speed of its electronic transmissions. The potential harm caused by an identity thief using the Internet is exponential," stated the report, produced by the National Fraud Center.

By the late-1990s, consumers and authorities alike were confronting the seriousness of this crime. In 1998, the Identity Theft and Assumption Deterrence Act was passed, which broadened the reach of the law to encompass misuse of documents and information, and it sharpened the judicial teeth of those prosecuting the offenders. With this Act, theft of someone's personal information with the aim to commit a crime became a federal offense that carried penalties of up to 15 years in prison and a maximum fine of $250,000. At the time, few states had implemented specific identity theft statutes. By 2005, the majority of states had done so to protect citizens from this pervasive crime. Since the turn of the century, identity theft has catapulted to the front of the line of concerns—it is a priority for law enforcement and the business world alike. Between 1998 and 2005, a series of further acts that aimed to fight the growing problem of identity theft was submitted for consideration to help protect privacy, especially in relation to the Internet and Internet fraud.

The Schumer-Nelson ID Theft Prevention Bill was introduced in April 2005 to help victims get their identities back and to impose regulations on data merchants to increase security. This bill seeks to achieve such goals as protecting Social Security numbers and requiring companies to inform customers if they transfer customer information to another party. The 2003 Fair and Accurate Credit Transaction Act (FACTA) tacked on new sections to the Fair Credit Reporting Act and helps consumers fight identity theft through privacy legislation, limits on information sharing, and consumer rights to disclosure. Congress has also required credit agencies to provide Americans with a free credit report each year to help people monitor their credit. In addition, FACTA made it possible for victims to have credit bureaus flag their accounts with fraud alerts after a theft. This legislation extends protection to military personnel and their information with the introduction of a 12-month active duty alert. Credit bureaus now add a notation to these files so any activity will be monitored and flagged to prevent fraud. Additional legislation, both approved and proposed, includes the Identity Theft Prevention Act, the Online Privacy Protection Act, the Identity Theft Victims Assistance Act, and the Internet False Identification Prevention Act—all of which make evident the growing concern over identity theft.

Penalties in Canada have generally been less harsh for identity thieves than in the United States, and legislation in Canada is lagging. "In fact, it's illegal to send a telegram in somebody else's name, but not to send an e-mail in somebody else's name. It's an example of how things need to be updated," says Maura Drew-Lytle, senior manager of media relations for the Canadian Bankers Association. Currently, impersonation with intent to defraud can land offenders up to 10 years in prison and fines and restitution determined by a judge's discretion. Identity thieves can also face fraud charges, which can carry a 10-year stint in prison. The federal government made some changes in 2001 to hike fines from $1,000 to $50,000 (with possible jail time) for using false identification when applying for documents such as birth certificates. Other initiatives including the Personal Information Protection and Electronic Documents Act (PIPEDA) and the Federal/Provincial/Territorial (FPT) Council on Identity are working to find better ways to safeguard identity documents and prevent identity theft. These tasks are challenging, especially given the fact that

Canada lacks an offense called "identity theft." Approximately 30 Criminal Code offenses and one National Defence Act offense offer some assistance with fighting identity theft, but organizations across Canada are calling for specific legislation so the country's law enforcement agencies can more effectively combat identity theft. Through the 1990s and up to the present day, technology has quickly surpassed North America's legislation, and governments are now scrambling to catch up.

Technology to Protect and Serve

With all its much-maligned tendencies, technology can be used for good instead of evil, and devices and programs are consistently being produced to help fight identity thieves. Antiphishing programs and services have been created to verify web site URLs and to alert users if a site is hiding its real address. These programs also monitor traffic on the Internet in an effort to locate and shut down phishing and pharming sites. Other gadgets, like "smart" cards, are part traditional plastic credit card and part computer. The chips contained in these cards store far more information than do magnetic strips: they include certain identifiers, like fingerprints, to confirm the user's identity at the checkout. While used widely in Europe, North America hasn't climbed on board with these cards yet, so obstacles must be overcome before this technology can provide effective protection for cardholders' identities. Fraud screening technology is also being used to monitor credit card use and flag unusual or suspicious activity, and consumer authentication technology is being introduced to make account information more secure online. Companies are quickly looking for ways to protect people's personal information, online and otherwise, in an effort to stop identity theft.

Perhaps by looking at the past and learning how identity thieves managed to collect and manipulate confidential personal data to commit identity theft, consumers will be better equipped to protect themselves, and law enforcement will be better able to track and prosecute offenders. Then North Americans can look ahead to what we can do tomorrow to fight identity theft and put these helpful strategies to good use in our everyday lives.

CHAPTER 6

The Future

The key to the future of fighting identity theft lies in protection. Law enforcement, government agencies, and private organizations are all banding together to spread the word about identity theft and educate consumers about what they can do for themselves. Consumers must learn how best to protect their information; businesses, in turn, must do all they can to protect the information they hold.

Only then will law enforcement be able to take a serious bite out of identity crimes.

There are a number of actions people can take to minimize the risk of their becoming victims of identity theft. When it comes to credit cards and debit cards, cardholders should be sure to sign their cards immediately upon receipt, and they should never loan these cards to anyone. Picking up card receipts and taking them with you, rather than leaving them on the restaurant table, with a cashier, or in the ATM is a good preventative measure against theft. Covering the keypad to protect your PIN code is also an easy way to thwart "shoulder surfers" who seek to peek at your information. The use of bank-specific ATM machines in high-traffic areas, rather than generic ATM boxes in obscure locations, is helpful, too. Further, careful examination of credit card statements to ensure no unusual or suspect charges exist on the account is one of the best ways to detect fraud quickly. And of course, if a credit card is stolen or lost, the cardholder should report it as soon as possible and cancel the card to close the window of opportunity for thieves.

Next, a little knowledge about the Internet goes a long way. Knowing what should appear on a web site could save you from entering information into a non-secure site. The image of a padlock—usually found in the bottom right corner of the page—should always be closed when you are entering personal information on the Internet. That closed padlock indicates the site is secure and should be safe to use. Phishing and pharming sites count on visitors' lack of awareness of these details that distinguish legitimate web pages from unlawful duplicates. Company logos provide another tool to distinguish between legitimate and illicit sites: at legitimate sites, you should be able to cut and paste or save a logo as a picture. If you cannot, this may be an indication the site is fraudulent. Also, check the web address that appears when you click to the new site. It should include the name of the company the site represents. If it's an eBay site, for example, it should incorporate some form of "www.ebay.com" and not merely display a list of numbers. As well, the address will often display "http" and, in brackets, an "s" that indicates a secure site.

Phishers are also notoriously bad spellers. Obvious spelling mistakes, extra spaces between words, irregular fonts, and other inconsistencies flag sites as fraudulent. (It is worth noting, however, that even legitimate sites might have an occasional mistake slip past editors.) The most important tip comes from banking institutions themselves. "Your bank will never send you an e-mail saying please update your account or verify your passwords," says Maura Drew-Lytle of the Canadian Bankers Association. The unsolicited nature of phishing e-mails should alert you that it's a fraud, and law enforcement urges people to immediately delete the message and notify the bank or organization represented in the scam. To avoid becoming a target for phishers, be selective about where you leave your e-mail address, and don't enter contests and surveys that may share your information.

Because social engineering is an important tool used by identity thieves, people need to be more cautious about what information they offer. Never dispense personal information over the telephone or by e-mail unless you are very certain of the legitimacy of the person or organization you are dealing with and with whom you initiated contact. If you aren't sure, ask questions and check up on the answers you receive to verify what the caller or e-mailer tells you. Better still, don't participate in e-mail or phone solicitations or draws in the first place—even those disguised as surveys or promotions that tempt you with the offer of prizes for participation. Whenever possible, ask to be removed from marketing call lists and opt out of these programs. While the United States is implementing this opt-out option, Canada is still in the planning phase of such an initiative.

Finally, consumers should monitor their credit closely to ensure no one is using their names fraudulently. Law enforcement suggests that everyone order his or her credit report once a year and read it over carefully to detect any unusual activities. However, taking this step once a year may not be frequent enough; many agents advise that you do this two or three times each year to be safe. "The only way you can effectively battle this is to monitor your credit. You almost have to monitor your account all the time," says Barry Elliot of PhoneBusters. Some companies allow consumers to monitor their credit 24 hours a day, 7 days a week, for a nominal monthly fee, depending on the country in which the company operates. Credit bureaus also provide these checks for free through the mail. As an alternative, some victims choose to freeze their accounts so no one can conduct a credit check on it. However, if the victims later want to apply for credit themselves, they must pay to unfreeze the account and then pay again to refreeze it once the check is complete.

As companies continue to develop different means and products that consumers can use to fend off identity thieves, some frustrated Americans are looking at a more radical solution: changing their Social Security numbers. In the past, swapping an old number for a new one was something undertaken only in the most extreme circumstances. To make this change, the Social Security Administration requires considerable documented proof of hardship, and it creates a logistical nightmare for the victim. They are required to track down every bank, utility company, credit card provider, and government agency that might hold the old number in their files and convince them to use the new one. A new card isn't a complete solution. It may lead to other problems, including the loss of evidence of a credit history, and, because the two numbers are linked to the holder's retirement, the new number may generate suspicion of fraud. In 2004, about 1,000 Americans received new Social Security numbers to distance themselves from the clutches of identity thieves.

Taking Care of Business

These prevention tips, along with those mentioned throughout this book, are all efforts we should incorporate into our lives to protect ourselves. But there is only so much consumers can do. The rest lies in the hands of businesses—many of whom exercise control over consumers' private information but have nevertheless suffered security breaches that generate serious risks for consumers and sometimes identity theft.

It costs money to implement the changes required to protect consumers and national economies from the consequences of identity theft. Most corporations aren't in a position—nor are they prepared—to invest the money necessary to ensure data banks and information remain secure. This reluctance further batters consumer confidence in such organizations. "You want to see why bills don't pass in Congress? Follow the money. You'll understand why legislators vote for very weak bills that favor industry instead of consumers. Follow the money," says Linda Foley of the Identity Theft Resource Center. Businesses, she says, need to acknowledge and own up to the fact that in many cases information has leaked beyond their control, and that they must notify consumers about breaches without hesitation or exception. The Security Breach Information Act of 2003 made California the first state to make it mandatory for companies to alert consumers to breaches. Those that don't inform consumers or don't lock down information are susceptible to civil lawsuits. It was because of this legislation that ChoicePoint and other security debacles were made public. By the middle of 2005, 35 states had followed suit—either by proposing or enacting security breach notification legislation. Ten states enacted laws that allowed consumers to restrict distribution of their credit reports, and 27 states had filed security freeze bills. In Canada, companies are not bound by law to report security breaches unless a criminal action has taken place. Such loopholes must be eliminated if North Americans are to have the opportunity to effectively protect themselves from lurking identity thieves. "Consumers have all realized that you can do as much as you want to protect your information, but if the business community doesn't step up to the plate, we're all lost," observes Linda Foley. The next battle, then, lies between the desires of consumers and the desires of business, and until these two entities collaborate, the only victors will be the criminals.

Identity Theft Timeline

1984 *2600* magazine launched

1992 Privacy Rights Clearinghouse established

1994 World Wide Web emerges

1995 Kevin Mitnick arrested for stealing credit card numbers

1998 Identity Theft and Assumption Deterrence Act passed.

Telemarketing Fraud Prevention Act signed into law.

Tiger Woods becomes identity theft victim.

1999 Identity Theft Act passed.

Federal Trade Commission starts collecting complaints from identity theft victims.

Identity Theft Resource Center founded.

Lou Harris-IBM Consumer Privacy survey reports that 94 percent of Americans think their personal information is vulnerable.

The Identity Theft Data Clearinghouse is established.

2000 Internet False Identification Prevention Act passed.

The Internet Fraud Complaint Center is created.

Identity theft tops FTC's list of consumer complaints.

Abraham Abdallah pleads guilty.

PhoneBusters streamlined as central source for identity theft prevention in Canada.

2001 TransUnion becomes the first credit reporting agency to develop a list of identity theft victims so preventative measures can be taken against credit fraud

CIBC erroneously sends personal information to American scrap yard

2002 The number of complaints of identity theft received by FTC doubles each year from 1999 to 2002.

New York announces bringing down Philip Cummings for massive identity theft.

2003 Coalition on Online Identity Theft formed by Information Technology Association of America and Microsoft Corp. along with several security vendors and e-commerce companies like eBay and Amazon.com.

United States Fair and Accurate Credit Transaction Act (FACTA) enacted.

CAN-SPAM Act (Controlling the Assault of Non-Solicited Pornography and Marketing Act) is passed to control spam e-mails.

Internet Fraud Complaint Center is renamed Internet Crime Complaint Center

2004 President George W. Bush signs the Identity Theft Penalty Enhancement Act.

Mortgage fraud grows five-fold since 2000 to 17,000 cases in the United States.

Identity Theft Assistance Center established.

2005 The Identity Theft Assistance Center begins sharing information with the FTC and law enforcement agencies across the country.

Phishing reaches record high in May.

ChoicePoint is one of many data brokers to announce security breaches this year.

Amazing Facts and Figures

- In 2004, the Federal Trade Commission fielded 246,570 complaints of identity theft. That number was up 52 percent from 2002.

- On average, victims spend about 600 hours and $1,600 (not including lost wages) recovering from identity theft over a number of years.

- Brightmail, a company that provides spam filters, estimated that in April 2004 alone, 3 billion phishing e-mails were sent around the world.

- Two studies conducted between July 2002 and July 2003 (by Gartner Research and Harris Interactive) indicated approximately 13.3 people are victimized by an identity thief every minute.

- The youngest recorded victim of identity theft is a three-week-old infant.

- Less than 1 in 700 cases of identity crime ends in a conviction.

- In the United States, Phoenix, Riverside-San Bernardino-Ontario, and Las Vegas are the areas most heavily hit by identity theft, according to per capita complaints. In Canada, nearly half of all fraudulent acts occur in or around Toronto.

- Cyber crimes are number three on the FBI's priority list. Only counterterrorism and counterintelligence rank higher.

- According to the Toronto Police Service, students are statistically the largest group victimized by identity thieves. They are often first-time credit card applicants and they tend to give out information more freely. Seniors, in comparison, are victimized for the greatest amount of money.

- In Canada, possession of multiple pieces of identification representing different people, possessing the personal information of another individual, and manufacturing or possessing "novelty" identification is not a crime. This is problematic given that these are all major elements of identity theft.

- A January 2005 poll conducted by WatchGuard Technologies, Inc. found that of the 686 Internet technology professionals questioned, two-thirds thought that spyware would be the top threat to network security over the coming year. Spyware affects about 91 percent of computers connected to the Internet.

• In 1999, a stalker named Liam Youens looked to Internet information service DocuSearch for the date of birth and Social Security number for Amy Boyer, a woman he had been obsessed with since they went to high school together a few years prior. DocuSearch was unable to give him the date of birth but handed over her Social Secutiry Number acquired from a credit agency for $45. He used this information to find Boyer and then murdered her. This pushed Congress to take action in the United States by proposing several laws to protect Social Security numbers.

• According to Canada's Social Insurance registry, the number of Social Insurance cards in circulation outnumbers the number of people in the country by about 1.4 million.

• In 2004, the FBI launched 150 investigations into malicious spammers that affected more than 150,000 victims and generated more than $215 million in losses. Many of these investigations were related to identity theft.

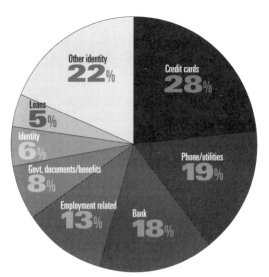

Newsweek magazine July 4, 2005

Other identity
22%

Loans
5%

Identity
6%

Govt. documents/benefits
8%

Employment related
13%

Credit cards
28%

Phone/utilities
19%

Bank
18%

Breakdown of complaints of fraud and identity theft in the U.S. for 2004. The cost of identity theft in the United States sits at around $53 billion.

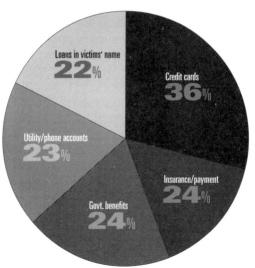

Consumer Measures Committee study July 2005

Loans in victims' name
22%

Utility/phone accounts
23%

Govt. benefits
24%

Credit cards
36%

Insurance/payment
24%

The Better Business Bureau of Canada estimates the cost of identity theft to consumers is around $2.5 billion. Total cost to the economy is around $5 billion per year.

Note: Percentages do not equal 100 percent due to some complainants being victims of more than one kind of identity theft

• In Canada, Visa and MasterCard experienced $163.18 million in fraud-related losses in 2004. While seemingly an outrageous amount, it represented less than one percent of the overall sales volume. Critics suggest that the overall profitability of credit card use may generate a lack of commitment on the part of those companies to battle identity theft.

• High-profile Canadian murderer Karla Homolka reportedly read *How to Disappear Completely and Never Be Found* by Doug Richmond in preparation for her 2005 release from prison. This book provides readers with tips about taking on another persona, including assuming the name of a deceased person, learning a new language, and subtly changing one's appearance.

• Between February and July 2005, reports of data breaches skyrocketed. More than 50 organizations, including universities, large corporations, financial institutions, data miners, and government agencies, released information about security vulnerabilities. Per incident, these breaches placed between 250 people and 40 million people at risk for identity theft.

What ID thieves want
Credit card numbers
CW2 security numbers (on back of credit card)
Credit reports
Social security number
Driver's licence number
ATM cards
Telephone calling cards
Mortgage details
Date of birth
Passwords/PINs
Home address
Phone numbers

Source: *Newsweek* magazine July 4, 2005

• Identity theft occurs seven times more frequently in the United States than in any other industrialized area, including the United Kingdom. In comparison, in continental Western Europe and Japan, identity theft is virtually unheard of.

What Others Say

"Identity thieves will exploit most-common names, such as Mary Smith or Peter Jones, names that are very easily spelled and easy to pronounce."

Constable Kathy Macdonald

These fraudsters are silver-tongued devils with no conscience—they want information and there's a lot of information out there. What separated Abdallah was his persistence."

Martin Biegelman, former U.S. Postal inspector on identity thief Abraham Abdallah

"It was a very frustrating experience. It's something I wouldn't wish on my worst enemy."

Shelby Laidlaw, identity theft victim

"Over the last nine years, criminals have gotten a better understanding of the power of information. Instead of selling drugs, so much can be made so quickly with identity theft, and the likelihood of getting caught is almost nil."

Rob Douglas of security consulting firm Privacy-Today

"Not doing anything [about identity theft] is not an option. It would be criminal to expose millions of additional people to the risk of their personal information falling into the hands of those who have no right to it. This is a David verses Goliath battle. We need a national notification standard now."

U.S. Senator Dianne Feinstein

"[Identity theft is] an awful crime, because in that crime, the criminal who's committing the crime is innocent until they're proven guilty, but the person who's the victim is guilty until they prove themselves innocent."

Frank Abagnale Jr., in a 2000 interview with Norman Swan

"As long as we live in a free country with ready access to information, and information is important—and we're not going to control that—criminals out there will find a way to obtain that information and commit identity theft."

Martin Biegelman, fraud investigator for large New York accounting firm BDO

"I have gained unauthorized access to computer systems at some of the largest corporations on the planet, and have successfully penetrated some of the most resilient computer systems ever developed … All of this was really to satisfy my own curiosity, see what I could do, and find out secret information about operating systems, cell phones, and anything else that stirred my curiosity."

Kevin Mitnick,
January 13, 2003, The Register

"The restless tide of e-commerce changes personal identity to a cipher. You stop being a person [and] start becoming pieces of data."

Nicholas Godson, fraud risk
consultant at Ernst and Young

"They make it so easy. They just tell you whatever you want to know. So many customers call for information, and they don't want to alienate them, so they try to please them. If you don't answer one question, they say 'Oh, don't worry about it. What is your Social Security number? What is your date of birth? What is your address?' Like you can't get that information."

Identity thief Abraham Abdallah in an interview with Mike Boal

"The defendant's crimes are everyone's worst nightmare when it comes to fears of privacy, identity theft and credit card liability from the proliferation of information available, intentionally and unintentionally, from the Internet and various institutions with which we do business daily."

Judge Deborah Batts when sentencing identity thief James Rinaldo Jackson

"The losses are not measured only in dollars, and identity thieves can steal the victim's financial reputation. Running up bills on credit card accounts that the victim never knew existed, the criminal can quickly damage a person's lifelong efforts to build and maintain a good credit rating."

President George W. Bush on signing the Identity Theft Penalty Enhancement Act in 2004

"We've evolved so quickly into the electronic age that it has now been circumvented by the criminals who are tremendously talented at defeating whatever safeguards have been put into place."

Staff Inspector Tony Crawford, Toronto Police Service Fraud Squad

"What bank robbery was to the Depression Age, identity theft is to the Information Age. Identity theft has become so pervasive and so out-of-hand, that we must make a real effort to prevent it before it happens. When a company like LexisNexis so badly underestimates its own ID theft breaches, it is clear that things are totally out of hand."

U.S. Senator Charles E. Schumer

"The truth is what I did 30 years ago is 200 times easier to do today than it was then, and 5 years from now will be 700 times easier than it is today, and that's because of one word: technology. … Today, sitting at home in an apartment with a PC, a scanner, a color printer, an inkjet printer, or a color copier, you can reproduce just about any type of document, including currency and paper."

Frank Abagnale Jr., in an interview with Norman Swan in 2000

"The Commission's experience is that fraud operators are always among the first to appreciate the potential of a new technology to exploit and deceive consumers."

Hugh Stevenson of the Federal Trade Commission's Bureau of Consumer Protection

"Changing one's Social Security number is the equivalent of trying to cure a patient by amputating a leg for a common cold. You have to separate yourself [from] everything that your Social Security number is attached to—all your professional records, your college transcripts, licensing, your credit history. If you change your Social Security number, you really have to change your driver's license and your name. You become a new person. In effect, you've created your victim's protection program."

Linda Foley in a 2004 interview with CBS News

Bibliography

Arata Jr., and J. Michael. *Preventing Identity Theft for Dummies.* Indianapolis, IN: Wiley Publishing, 2004.

Boal, Mark. "The Identity Addict: How a Restaurant Worker Without a High School Degree Stole Millions from the Richest People in America." *Playboy* (2004).

CNN.com. "National Fraud Center: Internet is Driving Identity Theft," by Jack McCarthy, (March 20, 2000).

Levy, Steven, and Brad Stone. "Grand Theft Identity." *Newsweek* (July 4, 2005): 38–47.

Roth, Daniel, and Stephanie Mehta. "Identity Theft: The Great Data Heist." *Fortune* (May 2005).

Saporito, Bill, Greg Fulton, and Mark Thompson. "Are Your Secrets Safe?" *Time Magazine* 165.10 (March 7, 2005).

Sullivan, Bob. *Your Evil Twin: Behind the Identity Theft Epidemic.* Indianapolis, IN: Wiley Publishing, 2004.

Swan, Norman. "Frank Abagnale: New Life." *Radio National Life Matters* interview with Frank Abagnale Jr. (March 17, 2000).

Weisman, Steve. *50 Ways to Protect Your Identity and Your Credit: Everything you Need to Know About Identity Theft, Credit Cards, Credit Repair, and Credit Reports.* New Jersey: Prentice Hall, 2005.

Welsh, Amanda. *The Identity Theft Protection Guide: Safeguard your Family, Protect your Privacy, Recover a Stolen Identity.* New York: St. Martin's Press, 2004.

Acknowledgments

So many people helped me to research and write this book. I'd like to thank everyone for their invaluable assistance, from my husband Bryce and mom Arlene, who gave me the time I needed to work without constant interruption from an energetic toddler named Carmen, to the knowledgeable and passionate professionals who dedicate their lives to fighting identity theft and helping people who have fallen victim to it.

I would first like to thank Constable Kathy Macdonald, Staff Sergeant Barry Elliot, and Staff Inspector Tony Crawford for taking time out of their very busy law enforcement schedules to school me on the ins and outs of identity theft and identity thieves. Their expertise was an enormous benefit to me and to this book. I would also like to thank Linda Foley for speaking to me about her experiences with identity theft and sharing her ideas and suggestions for the future if we are to control the spread of this crime. In addition, I'd like to thank Shelby Laidlaw for sharing with me her experiences with an identity thief and parting with her prized binder in which she keeps every detail about the crime and the process of clearing her name. Finally, thanks to Andrew Sayers for helping me collect information on this vast topic, making what I hope is a great resource.

I am also indebted to the amazing writers and journalists who have published works about identity theft before me. Their writings were a great inspiration to me and the information contained in them was a stepping stone to producing this book on identity theft. I'd also like to thank Associate Publisher Kara Turner for her advice and guidance throughout the process.

My sincerest thanks to you all.

Photo Credits